Complicite/Simon McBurney

The Encounter

Inspired by the novel *Amazon Beaming* by Petru Popescu

Complicite
The Encounter

Directed and performed by	**Simon McBurney**
Co-director	**Kirsty Housley**
Design	**Michael Levine**
Sound	**Gareth Fry** with **Pete Malkin**
Lighting	**Paul Anderson**
Projection	**Will Duke**
Associate Director	**Jemima James**
Production Manager	**Niall Black**
Company Stage Manager	**Caroline Moores**
Assistant Stage Manager	**Joanne Woolley**
Sound Operators	**Helen Skiera** and **Ella Wahlström**
Sound Supervisor	**Guy Coletta**
Production Engineer	**David Gregory**
Stage Supervisor	**Matt Davis**
Projection Supervisor	**Sam Hunt**
Lighting Supervisor	**Laurence Russell**
Design Assistant	**Lauren Tata**
Artistic Collaborators	**David Annen, Simon Dormandy, Naomi Frederick, Victoria Gould, Richard Katz, Tim McMullan, Tom Morris** and **Saskia Reeves**
Associate Producer	**Poppy Keeling**
Producer	**Judith Dimant**

The Encounter was originally co-produced with Edinburgh International Festival, the Barbican London, Onassis Cultural Centre – Athens, Schaubühne Berlin, Théâtre Vidy-Lausanne and Warwick Arts Centre.

It was first performed at the Edinburgh International Festival on 8 August 2015, before touring to Lausanne, Bristol and Warwick. In 2016 *The Encounter* played at the Barbican London, HOME Manchester, Onassis Cultural Centre – Athens, Brighton Festival, Oxford Playhouse, Wiener Festwochen, Vienna Festival, Holland Festival, Printemps des Comédiens, Montpellier and The Fourvière Nights, Lyon.

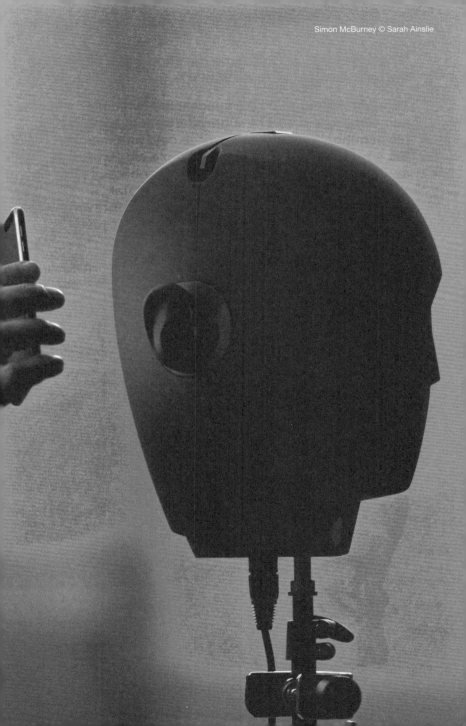

'There was always the same question when opening the unknown: What to do with it?

Thoughts, thoughts. Like spaceships, whirling somewhere in a sort of suborbital space. Lying in his hammock, shivering from the cold and hearing the sounds made by the tribespeople who were still awake, McIntyre was aware of a subsphere of his mind in which a different species of mental processes, less explicit and formal, were forever meeting, colliding, mixing. The tribe he had just encountered was part of them.'

Petru Popescu
from *Amazon Beaming*

Simon McBurney © Robbie Jack

Petru Popescu
Author of *Amazon Beaming*

I've always been fascinated with who we are as humans. But I grew up in Communist Romania. Dreams of exploration, of faraway lands or of the wilds of the mind were drastically discouraged in Communism.

In time, I became a turbulent dissident writer, then I ran away to America. Among my first writings in English, I co-wrote the movie *The Last Wave*, which dealt with an encounter of modern man and tribal man, in Australia. It became clear to me that I'd escaped from my locked-in homeland carrying a *dream of encounters* with pretty much any human, anywhere.

In the late 1980s, as I was sailing up the Amazon River – boom! – in the city of Manaus I met Loren McIntyre, the first Western discoverer of the Amazon River's source.

Loren was a traveller and *National Geographic* photographer. We became friends and he told me how he was captured in 1969 by the Mayoruna tribe, at that time thought to be extinct. Loren had rediscovered the 'cat people', but without a compass or any other instrument and speaking no common language, he remained virtually imprisoned by them for weeks. As they trekked upriver together, Loren witnessed a unique Mayoruna ritual: the tribesmen burned their belongings in order to go back in time, both chronologically – they really thought time would run backwards – and closer to the source of the river, which for them was 'Time's' own beginning. Belongings meant the present, and the present meant the oil prospectors who invaded their grounds and were erasing their tribal life.

The embers of our original fire are lit inside all of us. Blow on those embers; our flesh will awake and rise and dance in kinship like the early sapiens. The peaceful relay race from one man to another to another, that's what made us human.

All this may sound too prophetic and philosophical – when I first fell in love with Loren's story, it really was for its adventurous scenes, copious and various enough to fill the thick book I would eventually write. Simon McBurney read that book in 1994 and remained so beguiled that years later he decided to seek the stage rights for it.

'And how are you going to tell this story on stage?' I asked him, as I couldn't see how Simon would pour the Amazon waters across the stage in front of a live audience.

He wasn't sure yet, he replied.

Loren had trusted me with the book, I reminded myself. It was my turn now to trust the new relay runner.

In August 2015, I sat in a theatre at the Edinburgh Festival and along with the whole audience I put on a pair of headphones… A moan of rainforest, enormous, ingenious, stylised and yet so real that I felt I was crawling with jungle bugs, flowed out of the headphones and conquered my brain. And the actor/director, alone; he played Loren, he played headman Barnacle and interpreter Cambio, he played the deluging skies above soaked treetops and the stifling hot air on my own sweating skin, he played Loren's capture and discovery of the source, *and even the river flooding*, with evocative strength and suspense that made me gasp. How often does it happen that an author witnesses such an enrichment of his work?

My only regret is that Loren didn't get to see the show. He died in 2003, at age 86.

He would've been blown away.

Los Angeles, November 2015
Amazon Beaming *is available from pushkinpress.com*

We see only what we want to see
Simon McBurney

When making a piece of theatre I am, frequently, if not most of the time, in the dark. I truly do not know where we will end up.

— We're going to shut the door now and we'll open it again in twenty minutes. Is that okay?

— Yep, I guess.

— Have you ever sat in total silence? In the dark?

— I'll be fine.

As a result of spending sixty-three days in silence on a Vipassana retreat, Yuval Noah Harari, the acclaimed author of *Sapiens: A Brief History of Humankind*, proclaimed it the ideal tool with which to scientifically observe his own mind. He came to realise he had no idea who he really was and that the fictional story in his head, and the connection between that and reality, was extremely tenuous.

— Okay well… if you freak out then push this button and we'll open the door.

The vast door to the anechoic chamber, which is, as the name suggests, a room without echoes, at the Building Research Establishment (BRE) in Watford, closes definitively behind me.

The concrete walls are so thick no sound from the outside world enters your ear canals and the vast foam wedges that cover the walls absorb sound to such an extent that a clap becomes a tap.

I am in total darkness. And total silence. I don't mean the silence of three in the morning at home, or even the silence of the remotest place on Earth, I mean total silence.

My breathing sounds like a set of bellows; my heartbeat like an arrhythmic drum machine.

— Why am I here?

It is 40°C, my clothes are already sodden, although we have only been here an hour. Or have we? I've lost track of time and I have no battery on my phone. In fact I don't know why I have a phone at all given there is no signal here.

We are sitting in the house of Lourival Mayoruna, the headman or *Cacique* of Marajaí, a village of Mayoruna people deep in the Brazilian Amazon, an hour's flight west of Manaus and four hours by boat up the River Solimões.

Lourival, according to local protocol, talks to us as part of our welcome into the village – and has been doing so for the best part of an hour. The hut is crammed with people and sitting between us all like some twenty-first-century totem is a binaural head, the microphone that records in so-called '3D'.

Paul Heritage, head of People's Palace Projects, who has lived for more than twenty years in Brazil, translates as Lourival winds down...

— So you have come all this way and I have one question...

Lourival leans forward looking me in the eye.

— Why are you here?

I nervously lick the wet salt off my upper lip, and sweat stings my eyes as everyone's eyes turn towards me.

— I think you need to reply, says Paul.

The sounds of the forest and the village become extremely loud all of a sudden. I clear my throat.

The slight rising panic makes me realise the noise I am now hearing is the sound of fluids circulating in my head. And there is a high-pitched hiss caused by spontaneous firings of the auditory nerve. How long have I been sitting here in darkness? I squeeze my phone. Five minutes. I thought it was at least half an hour.

— Where are you going?

— To work on my show...

— What are you doing?

— Um... sitting in a dark silent room in Watford.

— Why?

— To see what it's like.

I look at my son. He is four. I'm not sure he buys this answer.

— When is Christmas?

— A long time. Several months. When it is winter, when it will be cold again.

— It was cold today.

— Yes, okay, but not very cold.

— Yes it was. I was cold.

— You're right, it was cold.

— How long is several months?

I mutter something about moons and loads of sleeps.

Maybe this high-pitched hiss generated by my auditory nerves is something more sinister. I should get my ears checked for tinnitus when I get out of here. How much longer?

— Forty-five minutes.

— What?

— You've been speaking for forty-five minutes.

— Good God.

I got it all, whispers Gareth my sound designer, who looks even more sodden than I do in the Amazonian heat, unplugging the totem.

I look round the room. Silence. I am not sure how it has gone down. In English, the word 'rehearsal' derives from 'hearse' which means to rake over. To prepare the ground. And one way for me to prepare has always been to perform or improvise a show I am making to those who have never heard it. Because the story is not the show. It is not even the performance that is the show. The show is made in the minds of the audience. I want to know what they see. What they hear. I look at Lourival. He smiles.

— We are moved by your story, he says. Your story about this man who was lost, but who survived. Your story is about many people, but it is also about us, the Mayoruna. And it tells us that others in this world know of the Mayoruna people. You tell the world that we have survived. Many have perished. We have survived. But whether we will all survive... that is another matter.

He laughs.

— So is it funny?

— What?

— Your performance.

Simon McBurney © Robbie Jack

My son examines me. I glance at him sideways. Draw in my breath.

The door suddenly creaks open and I am out in the Watford sunlight again, blinking. What greets me I don't expect. It shocks me. It is a roar. So loud I want to block my ears. Traffic, voices, machinery, planes... industrial, all-encompassing, unstoppable. The shock is that most of the time, I do not hear it because our auditory system blocks out our conscious mind. Our ears, without us asking, form a filter and help to create a 'normal' reality, but one in which we hear 'selectively'. As with our ears, so it is with all our senses. Our eyes, our sense of smell, every way in which we perceive the world creates a gap between what is actually happening and the story we make of it. We see only what we want to see...

The technician looks at me enquiringly.

— How was it?

— Disorientating.

— And how did that feel?

— Familiar.

August 2015

I've been working with Complicite since 1998, and I've travelled a fair few miles as we've made shows and toured them around the world. There have been many memorable moments, such as taking *Mnemonic* to Zenica, near Sarajevo, in 2003, a city that had been starved, literally and figuratively, by war, with ruin and decay palpable everywhere – our audience packed into every millimetre of space, such was their vociferous appetite for a culture that had been too long absent.

But no show has led me further away from a darkened theatre than *The Encounter*. I regularly work on shows set in exotic places that don't end up with me leaving the inside of the M25.

Amazon Beaming, the book that inspired the show, recounts how a *National Geographic* photographer, Loren McIntyre, went into the rainforest to take photos of the rarely seen Mayoruna tribe only to lose his way back. The normal approaches to adapt a book to the stage just didn't feel right. It needed an approach that could convey both the initial isolation of Loren McIntyre and the eventual way with which he could communicate with the tribe leader.

We explored the audience wearing headphones, separating them from each other, rather than the usual shared experience of being in an audience. This also allows a more intimate relationship with Simon, who can talk into a mic onstage which can be heard as if he is inside your head.

Our next step was to investigate binaural sound which is recorded on a type of microphone resembling a human head with a microphone in each of its ears. The effect of it is magical as it transposes the audience to where the head is, or has been, so they feel like they are on stage next to Simon. It is a unique sound and allows Simon to talk to and interact with the audience in a way that's not possible otherwise.

To tell the story we needed binaural sound effects, which are pretty rare – and that's how myself, Simon, photographer Chloe Courtney and Brazilian-based academic Paul Heritage found ourselves travelling to the Amazon rainforest, to spend four days living in a Mayorunan community – hearing their stories and travelling into the rainforest to record its sounds. Several hundred mosquito bites later, those recordings form the sonic bed for the show. Since then I've been binaurally recording Cessna aircraft in Surrey, mosquito colonies at the London School of Hygiene & Tropical Medicine, and leading a merry band of volunteers around Epping Forest – perversely, I got more mosquito bites in Epping Forest than I did at the mosquito colonies.

The Encounter is a devised show – the script came out of rehearsals as a process of experimentation and refinement. In fact, our press night in Edinburgh marked only the fifth time we'd ever run the show from start to finish. The show is, and will remain, in constant flux so we can change and refine the story as we go. To do this we have a team of unseen operators. Between them they respond fast to changes in the show, whether prearranged or as they happen during performance. Part of the process of making this show has been about learning how they can respond to Simon, to anticipate and to lead with sound, so that together we can act as one, and the division between storytelling and sound design are non-existent.

For me, this show started out in a rehearsal room five years ago with rudimentary technology as we explored the ideas that would form the show. We've harnessed the technology so it becomes invisible (but far from inaudible!) and indivisible from the process of telling the story.

Twenty years after Simon was given the book, six hundred pairs of wired headphones and two kilometres of headphone cable later – we have a show. For many productions the development time is spent working out what the story is you want to tell. For us, it has been about finding a new theatrical way to tell our story. We have developed a technique that uses technology to create intimacy, isolation and a little bit of magic, and will hopefully lift you out of your seat and take you as far away as this show has taken us.

October 2015

Gareth Fry recording in the Amazon Rainforest
© Chloe Courtney

The Encounter rehearsals © Sarah Ainslie

Binaural head in the Amazon Rainforest © Chloe Courtney

Memory and Identity
Paul Heritage

On 1 May 1500, Pêro Vaz de Caminha sent a letter to the King of Portugal informing him that Pedro Álvares Cabral had found the country that became known as Brazil. 515 years later, Paul Heritage has sent a reply...

Rua São João
Batista 105
Rio de Janeiro

July 2015

Dear Pêro Vaz de Caminha,

Let me introduce you to the theatre-maker Simon McBurney. In 2014 he began a journey to the land you first sighted on 22 April 1500 and described so vividly in your letter to Dom Manuel I. More than a letter, you wrote the birth certificate of Brazil, describing in extraordinary detail what happened during the first exchange with the people of the new world. Simon sends us now a performance that asks some of the same questions that have echoed down five centuries since you sent word of that first encounter.

In a rehearsal room in Bethnal Green in London, on an unseasonably cold afternoon in June 2015, I watch as Simon unfolds how he is going to enact the encounters that formed part of the journeys to the Amazon region of Brazil that we had undertaken together the previous year. Simon's rehearsal room is itself a place of encounter. Even though this is a monologue in the making, the room is full of people. The recorded voices of scientists, philosophers and political activists merge with the actual voices of the sound technicians and stage managers, overlaid with actor-friends who are there to interact with Simon as he develops, discards and discovers his ways of telling.

It is also a place where I hear again the sounds of Amazonian nights spent motionless in the darkness of a forest, recording a world that seemed intent on biting us to infinity. In the centre of a room, which is both hi-tech and a child's playpen, stands the ominous life-size dark grey head that had travelled with us on our visit to a Mayoruna village. Placed on a pole on a forest path at night, the head with its binaural technology had recorded Amazonian sounds that were now swirling a full 360° round us as we sit with our eyes closed in Bethnal Green. Just as when we read the words in your letter of five hundred years ago, Sr Vaz de Caminha, we are engaged in a collective act of imagination about an encounter that did not finish at that moment of its perception by one person, but is part of our consciousness now as we are sitting together.

Like so many of us, Simon had engaged with, imagined, created Brazil and its indigenous peoples for himself long before he visited it for the first time. What you describe in your letter about the meeting with those naked people in April 1500 became inscribed into the European imaginarium for the next five hundred years. Before he actually arrived for his first visit, Simon had been taken there through reading *Amazon Beaming*, Petru Popescu's account of the photographer Loren McIntyre's time spent with the Mayoruna people on his search for the source of the Amazon. After two decades of holding the book in his head and heart, Simon asked me to set up a visit to Brazil in order that he could meet indigenous people in a way that would enable him to begin work on adapting *Amazon Beaming* as a monologue that he could perform on stage.

You saw approximately five hundred people on that beach during ten days in 1500. They were just a tiny proportion of an indigenous population that numbered over five million at the time, made up of countless different peoples occupying the territory that became known as Brazil. By the time Simon stepped off a canoe in the River Solimões in March 2014, to be greeted by young girls in a Mayoruna village, over 90% of those peoples had been annihilated. Yet the depleted, decimated population that survives today is probably ten times greater than it was fifty years ago. It used to be assumed that indigenous people – the *índios* – had no future. War, legislation, disease, catechism and capitalism established a trajectory that seemed to indicate the unstoppable and inevitable extinction of the *índio* in Brazil. The end of the last indigenous groups was always supposed to be imminent and irresistible. But there we were in the State of Amazonas, two plane journeys and a couple of boat rides away from London, being led up the riverbank to a village that forms part of a growing Brazilian indigenous population now estimated to be approximately 900,000 people.

In the rehearsal room in Bethnal Green, Simon reminds us that McIntyre loses not only his watch but all sense of linear time during his stay with the Mayoruna, as described in *Amazon Beaming*. Simon plays with time in the construction of his performance, just as he did with his own schedule to steal the days we spent in

Amazonas and then later in the Xingu territories. Impossible as it was to carve out the weeks that would have been needed to travel to the Valley of Javarí, where the majority of the Mayoruna live on the borders between Brazil and Peru, we travelled to the village of Marajaí on the banks of the River Solimões where some of the tribe had relocated many decades earlier. It is there that Simon begins to experience and record the specifics of the forest while also confronting the villagers with the story of Loren McIntyre. He acts out with mime all that my translation cannot capture. The eighty-year-old *Cacique* (the head of the village) acknowledges with simple gestures and a nod of the head that he recognises the story Simon tells as part of the history of their people. Simon introduces the grey head that will capture the forest recordings, placing headphones on the *Cacique* and making birds and frogs appear round the old man, who reaches dreamily for all that Simon conjures up for him.

New stories form as we walk round the village over the next few days. The school with its internet connections, health centre and Cuban doctor, the condom wrapper on the path to the forest, the phone box and digital cameras. The original stories we brought with us are never enough, as we see the way in which this riverside community lives between worlds. *Índios* will not stay put in an unviable and inviolable myth of pure origin that has been created round them, but like all Amerindians across the Amazon region they know they must hold on to what has been taken from them by those they call the 'white man'. They are increasingly aware that this means taking responsibility for the production of their own identity. Just like Simon, they search for and record the dances, rituals and languages that they are in danger of losing. They are discovering their own ways of sharing and telling those stories using some of the same technologies as the 'white man'. They want to participate in the modern world – to be Brazilian – so long as their identity and differences are respected. All the complexities of those first ten days of April 1500, when Brazil was born in the exchange that took place between two cultures, are still being played out in the village of Marajaí.

The mono-motor Cessna that took us to the Xingu five months later was a necessity imposed by the limited time we had to make the trip. We had been invited to the Xingu funeral ritual known as the Kuarup, which in August 2014 was going to take place in the village of the Yawalapiti. Carved out of the southern part of the Amazon region, the Xingu is bigger than Belgium and was created by the Brazilian government as a territory for indigenous peoples to protect them from the encroachment of 'progress' that would have destroyed their lands and therefore their cultures. The two-and-a-half-hour flight we made from Goiânia, on the central plains of Brazil, could surely not have been so very different from the journey made by the Villas-Bôas brothers who had fought so hard to establish the Xingu Park in the 1950s. We felt the same intense drone of the engines, the same unnerving sway of the plane as it is caught by air currents, bouncing as ferociously as if we were arriving on one of the dusty, untarmacked tracks that cut through the forest below.

The view that we saw for the first hour, of course, was noticeably different from what the Villas-Bôas brothers would have seen fifty years earlier. Leaving the jagged urban landscape of Goiânia – home to those whose lives and disproportionate incomes depend on Brazil's agroeconomy – we rise 10,000 metres above the uninterrupted soya fields that have gorged the land. This soya will feed cattle that produce meat which is served at dinner tables all over Europe and North America. It will be nurtured with pulverised fish farmed from the oceans, and the toxic chemicals that enable this crop to proliferate on the unforgiving Brazilian savannah will seep deep into the earth and rivers. As we reach the Xingu there is an abrupt, exact line like a scar, which separates modern Brazil from the ancient forest. The line marks the point where the mono-colour soya fields give way to the multiple greens of the forest panoply and the interconnecting loops of the rivers, broken only by irregular red-dirt tracks that occasionally lead to the vast circular forms of the Xingu villages. These are the *aldeias* of the nine different ethnic groups that inhabit the territory of the Upper Xingu.

We land on one of the dusty roads that has served as an airstrip since the Villas-Bôas brothers first arrived there in the 1930s. An *índio*, blackened with jenipapo and naked apart from his waistband, helps us step across the wing of the plane and down onto the Xingu lands for the first time. It is difficult for me not to think of your landing, Pêro Vaz de Caminha, and the Guarani *índios* who put down their weapons to help you from the rowing boats that brought you ashore from the Portuguese galleons. Simon and I remove our many bags of food, clothes, hammocks and presents to be greeted by the representative of FUNAI, the government's agency for indigenous affairs. Simon is already attached to his recording equipment to capture the sound of the Cessna as it immediately prepares to take off and leave us in such unfamiliar and yet very welcome territory.

Lourival and Joaquina, Complicite's hosts in Marajai, listening to the binaural head © Chloe Courtney

A kombi van stripped of most of its seats takes us for thirty minutes down a dusty, suspension-busting road to reach the final stage of our journey as the sun begins its rapid descent. We are left on the edge of a mighty circle of nine long, tall *ocas* – the same huts that you recorded in your letter over five hundred years ago. We are staying with Pikakumã and his wife Iamoni, who step out to greet us. Iamoni leads us into the darkened, cool air of their *oca*. Wordlessly she accepts the beads, fish-hooks and wool that we have been instructed to bring, and Pikakumã shows us how to attach our hammocks between the wooden stakes that rise up the arching walls and the central pole of the hut.

From the moving uncertainty of my hammock I watch two musicians enter, naked yet in full ceremonial dress, with wooden flutes stretching almost two metres in front of them, suspended just above the earthen floor as they breathe long across the wide opening that hangs from their lips. The low echoing sounds of these decorated flutes will reverberate across the *ocas* until the final moments before we leave four days later. Simon lies in the hammock beside me, watching, listening, writing, recording. Being there. Tomorrow at 4 a.m. he will walk towards the sunrise across the dusty oval of the central ground between the *ocas* and whisper, 'the best awakening of my life'.

The Kuarup introduces us to the rituals of the Xingu. There is no fixed liturgy but a flux and flow of repeated actions, music and dances; it will be difficult for us to understand how and why a movement ends or when another begins. The Xingu conjure a world of spirits that elude, spirits that attack, spirits that need to be appeased, spirits that evade and invade lives. There is spirituality in the struggles of the young men fighting, yet their dusty, ferocious two-minute wrestling bouts also offer a ludic attraction within the ritual. Spirituality is invoked through struggles that are part of the memory and identity of a people. Throughout the four days, other villagers are summoned and arrive from afar by boat, bicycle, motorbike and on foot to be part of this year's Kuarup. There is a spiritual insecurity to be found in the Xingu as they gather to celebrate their funeral ritual: a sense of still trying to discover what life is and what it is about. Perhaps that is what has drawn Simon here. It is part of his struggle and his destiny, just like the journey that Popescu traces for McIntyre in *Amazon Beaming*. A journey to a place where everything converges.

Although you did not survive the long journey back home to Lisbon, Pêro Vaz de Caminha, your letter reached its destination and has continued to speak to us across the centuries of an encounter in April 1500 that defined both a new world and our destiny. Globalisation seemingly brings people and lands ever closer, and yet our translations and exchanges become ever more disjunctured as we inhabit and construct places of exclusion where nothing converges. Like you, Simon McBurney is a traveller who navigates, deciphers and translates our incommensurable worlds.

The *índios* on that faraway shore in 1500 remain silent in the pages of your letter. But the twenty-first-century *índio* is broadcasting, directing films, writing poetry and posting on Facebook. They were photographing Simon McBurney on their iPhones as he recorded their dances and they were not there to be discovered. As the contemporary poet Davi Kopenawa Yanomami writes (cited in *Amazônia*: catalogue for an exhibition by Gringo Cardia; Fare Arte, 2004):

> ...I am a son of the ancient Yanomamis
> I live in the forest where my people have lived since I was born
> and I don't tell white men that I discovered it!
>
> It has always been here, before me.
> I don't say: 'I discovered the sky!'
> I don't say: 'I discovered the fish, I discovered the hunting!'
>
> They were always there from the beginning of time.
> I simply say that I eat them, that's all.

Let all our encounters be a mutual feast.

A kiss of your hand,
Paul Heritage

Paul Heritage is Professor of Drama and Performance and Director of People's Palace Projects, Queen Mary University of London.

Simon McBurney © Robbie Jack

Designer Michael Levine in BRE anechoic chamber
© Simon McBurney

Binaural head in Epping Forest © Sarah Ainslie

Simon McBurney © Robbie Jack

Complicite

'a company who are incapable of remaining within known theatrical boundaries' *Independent*

Since it was founded in 1983, Complicite has performed worldwide, winning over fifty major theatre awards.

Recent work includes *Lionboy*, its first show for children and families, *The Master and Margarita*, *Shun-kin*, co-produced the Setagaya Public Theatre, Tokyo, and *A Disappearing Number*, winner of the 2007 Olivier Award for Best New Play. Alongside its productions, Complicite runs an award-winning Creative Learning programme, with recent projects including *Like Mother, Like Daughter* and *Tea*.

THE ENCOUNTER

Complicite/Simon McBurney

Inspired by *Amazon Beaming*
by Petru Popescu

Note on the Text

The Encounter is performed by one actor and two sound operators. During the introduction the audience are asked to put on a set of headphones, which they then wear for the duration of the performance. Everything they hear is through these headphones. The actor uses a range of microphones that can be modified to create the voice of Loren McIntyre and other characters. The actor also creates a variety of live foley sound effects onstage, and uses loop pedals to create exterior soundscapes and the interior worlds of the characters. The performer also plays some sound and audio recordings live through their mobile phone, iPod, and various speakers. All sounds created or played onstage are picked up and relayed to the audience's headphones through a variety of onstage microphones, one of which is binaural.

Other sound is played and mixed live by two operators who in part improvise in reaction to the performer onstage.

In this text only the most basic indication is given as to which microphones, loop pedals and other effects are used, and when. Most of these decisions have been left for each performer and company to discover.

Characters

ACTOR, *originally played by Simon McBurney*

LOREN McINTYRE, *a* National Geographic *photographer, aged fifty-two*

PILOT, *flies Loren into the Javari in 1969*

CAMBIO, *a Mayoruna shaman who speaks both Mayoruna and Portuguese*

BARNACLE, *this is pre-recorded, and heard as Loren's voice reverberating in his own head. It will be characterised throughout the script as* 'BARNACLE (LOREN *voice-over*)'

RECORDED VOICES

During the introduction, and throughout the piece, we hear the voices of people that Simon McBurney discussed aspects of this show and related subjects with. In order of appearance, they are:

NOMA McBURNEY, *Simon McBurney's daughter, aged five*

MARCUS DU SAUTOY, *Simonyi Professor for the Public Understanding of Science and Professor of Mathematics at the University of Oxford*

REBECCA SPOONER, *campaigner at Survival International, the global movement for tribal peoples' rights*

PETRU POPESCU, *author of* Amazon Beaming

IRIS FRIEDMAN, *writer, and wife of Petru Popescu*

IAIN McGILCHRIST, *psychiatrist and philosopher*

STEVEN ROSE, *Emeritus Professor of Biology and Neurobiology at the Open University and Gresham College, London*

GEORGE MARSHALL, *climate-change communications specialist, co-founder of Climate Outreach and author of* Don't Even Think About It: Why Our Brains Are Wired to Ignore Climate Change

JESS WORTH, *writer and activist, campaigner with direct-action theatre group 'BP or not BP?' to end oil sponsorship of the arts*

DAVID FARMER, *oceanographer*

NIXIWAKA YAWANAWA, *member of the Yawanawa tribe, currently living in Bath. He is the voice of himself and the Mayoruna*

ROMEO CORISEPA DREVE, *member of the Harakmbut tribe, currently living in Exeter. He is the voice of Barnacle in Mayoruna*

This text went to press before the end of rehearsals and so may differ slightly from the play as performed.

1. The Beginning

As the audience enters, it seems there is almost nothing on stage. Anechoic soundproofing covers the back wall, but the stage should appear prosaic to the point of dullness.

Onstage are various speakers and microphones. A desk and chair are downstage-right. A binaural head is centre stage, facing the audience.

Multi-packs of water bottles are placed at various spots around the stage.

The opening section is partly improvised.

The ACTOR *invites the audience to turn their telephones off, and from this simple announcement begins to talk to them in a conversational manner that suggests the show has not really yet begun. This draws the audience into another kind of attention, through the description of how the evening will unfold.*

ACTOR. My daughter is five. She doesn't believe I work at night, so I'm going to take a photo of you all on my iPhone to prove I was really here. I have more photographs of my children here than there are photographs of my entire life. And these are just the ones I've taken in the last week. And there are more photographs on a single page of my phone than I have of the whole of my father's childhood. Looking at these pictures of my children, I feel such a sense of responsibility. Because when they look at them, they feel as though they're looking back at their whole lives.

But it is not their lives, it is only a story. And I worry they'll mistake this for reality, just as we all mistake stories for reality.

There's something uniquely human about telling stories. You might say that stories are what have allowed the human race to thrive. Stories, fiction, are how we explain, organise and agree on the meaning of our lives.

For example, two men who have never met might go to war together to fight and die for something called the United Kingdom. But the United Kingston does not exist. It's a fictional idea that helps us organise ourselves into… what?

Two lawyers will fight to defend someone they don't know because they both believe in the existence of the law, justice and human rights. But these things don't exist. They're fictions. Stories.

They don't exist outside the collective imagination, but they allow us to organise ourselves by forming narratives we can all agree on wherever we are. They shape everything we see and believe in.

That is why I feel so responsible for the stories I tell my children…

I remember my father reading me bedtime stories as a child that transported me to other places and times. And that was how, for the first time, I started to get inside someone else's head, and imagine what their experiences felt like.

And now I get into bed with my children at night, and tell them stories in the same way. I watch them empathising with the characters, discovering what connects and separates them from other people, other worlds. It is an intimate process.

It seems empathy and proximity are connected, so I'd like to get closer to you. Can you put your headphones on?

The following text is spoken into a microphone and is heard by the audience through their individual headphones. From now on, all narration, dialogue and other text, as well as all sound effects, are heard by the audience through the headphones.

So now instead of shouting I can be as close to you as I am to my children. Closer in fact, because now, instead of whispering in your ear, I am in the middle of your head.

I would like to check your headphones are all working, I will take a walk from one side of your head to the other, without even moving.

The sound the audience hears moves to the left ear.

I am now in your left ear, and now... I will move across to the right side.

The sound moves across towards the right ear. A very brief pause in case any audience members still have their headphones the wrong way round.

This is all being manipulated by technicians at the sound desk, but you have the feeling that my voice has 'walked across' your brain. I have not, but you 'feel' that I have.

Now you will feel that my voice is getting lower in pitch. It is not. It is simply being modified by a pitch modifier, also operated from the sound desk behind you. But it does appear that my voice has lowered.

The following is spoken into a different microphone, with voice-modification effects pitching the voice lower.

LOREN. And as my voice is getting lower, I too begin to 'feel' not quite myself. It feels more comfortable to me to speak now with an American accent. And this is the voice I will adopt for the principal character in the piece, the photographer Loren McIntyre. Loren McIntyre whose story unfolds in 1969. Here he is. And now you begin to accept this pitch as truly my own voice. So much so that when I speak in my 'normal' voice, the one I first used...

The ACTOR *moves to the other microphone which is not pitch modified.*

ACTOR. Of course I immediately sound like Mickey Mouse.

My voice was modified in pitch. But how might we also play similarly with the idea of space?

The binaural head is now turned on, picking up the ACTOR*'s voice and the acoustics of the space. The following is heard binaurally.*

To do so I'm going to use another microphone, a binaural microphone, which imitates the human head. It places you aurally right here on the stage. As if these ears were yours. It's as if you were standing onstage with me.

It's a somewhat skewed impression because the right ear is your left ear and the left ear is your right ear. So I'm just going to turn it around so it's in the right configuration.

The head is turned to face upstage.

Now what I would like you to do is close your eyes. I'm going to take a little walk, around your head. You should have the impression that I really am beside you. This is not digital manipulation, this is what I'm really doing. Now I'm getting a little bit too close, maybe a little too intimate.

I'm a little bit dry, so I think I'll have some water.

Pours and drinks water.

That's better.

And to give you a sense of how the brain mistakes fiction for reality, I'm going to breathe into your ear and it will literally start to heat up.

Breathes.

Oh and there's just a little hair here that I'll get for you. And while I'm here I think I'll give you a little haircut.

Snips the scissors around the binaural head.

SFX on small hand-held speaker: a mosquito flying around the head.

And now there's this damned mosquito flying around.

Please open your eyes.

The ACTOR *is standing with a speaker in their hand.*

And there's no mosquito. There's just this speaker. It sounds real, but it is in fact just a –

The following is pre-recorded, although that might not be immediately obvious.

RECORDING. – *speaker which is producing the sound of the mosquito. And as you look at it, the sound seems less convincing, simply because your eyes are telling you that you are listening to a recording. And in fact, it's not even a real mosquito, but a recording of someone blowing on a piece of paper and a comb…* (*Continues.*)

LIVE. And what you've probably realised by now is that this too is a recording. This is something that happened six months ago, when we were working on the show. Excuse me, can you turn the mosquito off now.

RECORDING. *What?*

LIVE. Can you turn that off; it's really annoying.

RECORDING. *You want me to turn it off?*

LIVE. Yes, it's really annoying.

RECORDING. *Okay.*

LIVE. Thank you. My voice over there is a recording, he doesn't exist.

RECORDING. *What do you mean I don't exist?*

LIVE. You're not real.

RECORDING. *Well, of course I'm real.*

LIVE. He's a recording from the past.

RECORDING. *No, I'm in the present and you're in the future!*

LIVE. No you're in the past and I'm the present.

RECORDING. *Well okay, I'm in the past. Shall we swap sides?*

LIVE. Okay, no problem. That's not going to affect causality.

RECORDING. *So, where are you?*

LIVE. I'm on stage, at [name of theatre].

RECORDING. *Oh my god! Should I be worried?*

LIVE. No, not particularly.

RECORDING. *How many people are there?*

LIVE. Quite a few.

RECORDING. *How's it going?*

LIVE. Well, they seem to be enjoying it.

RECORDING. *I'll just carry on talking then. Since I'm now clearly somewhere in the past, and I don't really exist. Well actually, I think I do, because your past is probably more important to you than your present. And actually your past is probably more present to you than anything else. It's created who you are. But your past is also a story. And we use that story to try to predict the future. So we'll look back and say…*

The recorded voice continues as the ACTOR *onstage begins to speak over it.*

LIVE. That's true. We wouldn't be who we are without all the things that we've experienced. Could we even be conscious without our pasts, I mean, is consciousness possible without memory? I think not.

This was recorded six months ago in my flat.

Over here is my desk. And here is a window…

Opens the window and the sound of the street comes rushing in.

Closes the window.

That was the street outside my flat in London. And there's a sink here. I'll just go and wash my hands…

SFX: water running.

You should hear that just behind your right ear.

The following conversation is between the ACTOR, *live, and Noma McBurney, aged five, recorded at home.*

NOMA. *Dada, who are you talking to?*

ACTOR. And that's my daughter, Noma. I'm not talking to anybody, sweetie.

NOMA. *Yes, you are!*

ACTOR. No I'm not. Well, I am in a way…

NOMA. *But there's nobody there!*

ACTOR. That's true, there's nobody there.

NOMA. *Dada, how long is this head going to be in our house?*

ACTOR. Well, sweetie, it's just while Mama's away. I'm going to record you, just for this evening.

NOMA. *Where's Mama?*

ACTOR. Mama's just gone away for a couple of days, my sweetie.

NOMA. *Daisy, Daisy, give me your answer do. I'm half-crazy...* (*Continues*.)

ACTOR. That's a recording I made about a year ago. When she was five. She's six now. So we've got three times going on. We've got this time, present. Six months ago there's me remembering stuff, and then we've got a year ago when I recorded my daughter. But is that possible? Surely we only live in one time? This is just something we've achieved with some sound recordings. Maybe...

Marcus, would you like a cup of coffee?

The following is a conversation between the ACTOR, *live, and Marcus du Sautoy, recorded. All other times are still 'running' concurrently.*

MARCUS. *No, I've already had one, thanks.*

ACTOR. So, Marcus, you're a scientist. I want to ask you about time. Leaving aside whether time even exists or not, I wanted to ask if this time that we're living in is the only time that there is? Is it possible that time is not just a single thing that we experience, there might be more than one time at any given moment?

MARCUS. *Yes, there are models of time where there are many kind of dimensions of time. So we tend to think of time as one-dimensional, a line that we're sort of running, but there are models where time is two-dimensional...* (*Continues*.)

ACTOR. And this is a conversation I had about two years ago with Marcus du Sautoy, who is the Simonyi Professor of Scientific Knowledge at Oxford University and he said that yes, the latest thinking about time is that it is possible that more than one time can be running parallel to this one. This is how many physicists are now thinking. But of course one of the dominant feelings about time is that it's just a fiction; a story and it doesn't exist. Something that we have made up in order to –

The ACTOR*'s phone rings.*

– make sense of the world. Oh my god, I knew this would happen. I'm the only person who hasn't turned their phone off. Just hang on one moment whilst I get rid of this.

The ACTOR *answers the phone. The following is pre-recorded.*

Oh, Rebecca. Thank you so much for calling me back. Yes, that's right. About the piece I'm making. I really want to talk to you about your experiences with the Mayoruna in Brazil and Peru.

The ACTOR *resumes talking to us live, over the recording of themself and Rebecca in the past.*

And of course as you've already guessed that's also a recording. I was talking to a woman – and that's about two-and-a-half, three years ago – called Rebecca Spooner from Survival International, an organisation that looks after the rights of indigenous people all over the world.

Gradually we encounter other voices, of activists, philosophers, writers, and scientists, whose words begin to layer over the top of one another eventually forming a cacophony that rises and rises until it becomes the sound of a machine, a motor, an engine that is in fact the engine of a Cessna plane…

2. Over the Ocean Forest

SFX: interior of a Cessna aeroplane.

A PILOT *is flying. Behind him sits Loren McIntyre. The text of Loren McIntyre is pre-recorded using the pitch-down voice modification demonstrated in the introduction. The* ACTOR, *shouting over the engine sound, plays the* PILOT.

PILOT. We can't go on for much longer. We have to land soon.

LOREN. *Where's the village? If this is the area where you saw the village, let's go on as long as we can. Make sure at least it's still there.*

PILOT. In two minutes I have to turn back or we'll be out of fuel.

LOREN. *First find that village. Climb a little higher and see where we are.*

The sound of the plane banking rises. The ACTOR *turns.*

PILOT. I'm looking. I can't… There it is! You see that clearing?

LOREN. *Let's go over twice.*

PILOT. Alright.

LOREN. *Let's do it twice. They'll have seen planes before, and know we're heading upstream.*

SFX on small hand-held speaker: sound of plane flying. The speaker is moved over the binaural head. The audience hear it as a plane flying overhead.

Music.

SFX: loud sound of a plane passing overhead. The ACTOR *turns, stands, hat off, stick in hand: a man on the ground looking up at the sky.*

The ACTOR *puts their hat back on and moves to the binaural head to begin their narration.*

ACTOR. They were hurtling along over jungle treetops at a hundred miles an hour in a Cessna 206 floatplane. The limit of their flying time was nine hours, of which four and a half had already elapsed. They were looking for somewhere to land. The river was a runway. But underneath the river were hidden logs.

PILOT. I can't see anywhere to land!

LOREN. *Not too far. Every minute of flight time is a day on foot, remember.*

PILOT. I know. I'm looking for a clear stretch.

LOREN. *You see that beach down there?*

PILOT. Yeah. I'll set her down.

SFX: plane coming in to land.

LOREN. *I'll set up camp there and you can pick me up in two or three days.*

PILOT. Okay. Here we go… She's down.

SFX: plane landing on water.

Music continues.

The ACTOR *takes a gulp of water from a large bottle, then uses it to create the sound of lapping, splashing water. By moving around the binaural head, this sound is looped to run under the next section of narration.*

ACTOR. The pilot helped Loren McIntyre jump ashore into the shallows, gave him his waterproofed sacks. Within minutes, the heat enveloped him like a fog. The plane taxied back. The drone of the engine faded. Loren McIntyre was totally alone. Four hundred miles of jungle in every direction. Four hundred miles from what he called civilisation.

He was used to it, he'd been photographing in the rainforest for more than twenty-five years. He prepared his cameras, checked his film. A well-organised ritual. The looming forest projected an air of distrust, watching him.

Mahoganies. Cedars. Palo sangres – wood so heavy it refused to float and red it justified the name blood trees. Huacapus – their wood so hard that nails wouldn't penetrate them. Giant Sumaúmas, and lupunas – known as river lighthouses because boatmen used them as landmarks.

All these, and their retinue of parasites, bromeliads, vines, mosses, bark mushrooms, exuded a tense, febrile stillness, like a beast waiting to ambush its prey.

He washed in the river, prepared a simple meal and as the light began to fade, he climbed into his hammock, pulled out a notebook, a virgin notebook and a virgin page, and began to write in an accurate, slightly slanting hand.

The following is spoken live, into the pitched-down microphone.

LOREN. October 20th, 1969.

I'm here because of the Mayoruna. The cat people. Mayoruna. Mayoruna. What a mystery there is in names. How does a tribe come to name itself? How do words become formed; how do they think them up, combining certain sounds and not others? How did they choose which one they thought to be real? What they played with until habit and general acceptance confirmed them into the general vocabulary. Mayoruna. In their language, it means *people*. (*Looped*.)

Petru recording, played on the ACTOR*'s phone into the binaural head.*

PETRU. *He was incredible to be around, because he had a million stories that… most of them will not be made into anything. I mean, he had met people, he had been this, he had been that. He had travelled extensively since he was a kid. He started as a sailor. Then he served in the US navy. So he was a fantastic character.*

ACTOR. *He was charismatic?*

PETRU. *Oh yes. In a sort of subtle, moderate way that was not apparent right from the beginning. He was not always making big gestures, he was always taking pictures.*

IRIS. *He was like an American cowboy.*

SFX: door creaking open. The following is a conversation between the ACTOR, *live, and a child, Noma McBurney, recorded aged five.*

ACTOR. Oh my sweetie, look, it's…

NOMA. *I can't sleep.*

ACTOR. Listen, I'm in the middle of working.

NOMA. *Who's like an American Cowboy?*

ACTOR. Well… I'm just listening to Petru talk about Loren McIntyre. You remember Petru?

NOMA. *What animals are in the jungle?*

ACTOR. We've been through all this already. There are jaguars, and monkeys, and birds…

NOMA. *What do they sound like?*

ACTOR. You have to go to bed, my darling. Look okay, I'll do it one more time, then you have to go to sleep. Do you promise?

NOMA. *Yes.*

> *The* ACTOR *creates the sound of the jungle, looping one animal/bird/insect sound over another by walking around the binaural head.*

3. First Contact

Looped animal sounds continue.

All of the following text is delivered live, alternating between the ACTOR *and* LOREN.

ACTOR. Daybreak, he was awakened as if by a silent clock. He bathed in the river, dressed, cooked himself some oatmeal. Slipped three rolls of film into his pocket and walked up the beach towards the giant lupunas. He started to walk around it, when somehow, on the screen of his mind:

LOREN. You are not alone.

ACTOR. He had a sensation of presence and almost instantaneously saw a young man in the forest, naked. Two plots of red urucu on his cheeks. Behind him appeared a boy, another man and a third, with a dead red howler monkey on his back. Spines bristled out of their lips, and there was no doubt that these people were Mayoruna.

LOREN. Cat people.

ACTOR. Loren McIntrye looked at them. They looked at him. His camera, a Minolta, weighed on his chest.

LOREN. Okay… I could shoot from the hip. No, let's get it through the viewfinder.

ACTOR. He raised the camera. No reaction. This was the instant when things could go either way, towards friendliness or hostility. He looked at them. They looked at him. He knew the Mayoruna had never been successfully acculturated, and at the turn of the century, as the rubber boom brought more intrusion and conflict to upper Amazonia, they had simply plunged into the forest and disappeared. And now they were reappearing, undoubtedly still carrying memories of conflict, brutality, and bloodshed. He looked at them. They looked at him. The moment was wonderful and unrepeatable.

SFX: camera shutter.

LOREN. First contact. What a shot, that's great. Ideal first contact.

ACTOR. They stood. Looking at each other. And then suddenly, they turned.

The ACTOR *creates the sound of walking on leaves using a box of loose videotape. SFX is looped. Sound of breathing, looped.*

Music.

During the following, the ACTOR *takes photos. Repeated SFX: camera shutter.*

LOREN. Hang on, fellas!

ACTOR. They were disappearing into the forest. What to do now?

LOREN. Okay, it seems okay. I'll follow them.

ACTOR. The path followed a twisting trail, deviating right or left practically every few steps.

The river, which had been straight behind him was now lost. He didn't remember where it was but he didn't care.

LOREN. Great light!

ACTOR. He hurried on and caught up with them again.

LOREN. Change the roll…

SFX: roll of film being changed.

ACTOR. He was far too busy photographing to break off twigs and mark the trail.

He was excited and he expected a village to appear at any minute.

Then he glanced at his wristwatch. He hardly ever checked his watch in the forest; there was no reason to do so. He'd been walking for more than an hour.

LOREN. I may not be able to retrace my steps to the river. I'm sure their village is not far.

ACTOR. But the truth was, that being so fascinated with the Mayoruna, he'd simply forgotten to mark his passage as he normally did. He was so far in the jungle he had no way of getting back. Time passed. Five, ten, twenty minutes later, there was still no village.

LOREN. Just think about the pictures. Keep your mind on the *pictures. (Looped.)*

This could be it. Your chance at the big one.

SFX: camera shutter.

4. Encountering the Village

ACTOR. Suddenly the trees pulled back. Staring in surprise, Loren stumbled. A narrow horizon of huts, perhaps six, seven, eight or nine at a glance. It was a village, but everything was half-finished. A provisional air hung about the place.

The man with red cheeks, the leader of the group he had followed, turned to stare at him with eyes like black bullets. The little boy walked towards Loren, curious.

RED CHEEKS. Tuti!

ACTOR. Was that the boy's name? Or was it a warning? And then he was immediately surrounded by tribespeople. They showed their surprise by silence and an almost solemn expression. They stood all around him.

LOREN. Hablas Español? Fala Português? Me llamó Loren.

ACTOR. There was no response. Strange, as over the years even marginal tribes had borrowed from Spanish and Portuguese.

People got very close to him, and suddenly a man with a conical hat of leaves hurried over, and then without being physically pushed, he was made to advance along the body of a tree, which had fallen through the clearing, towards a hut, as unassuming as all the others. In front of it was a man with a headdress of white egret feathers, sat on a carved stool. The headman, if headman he was, had dry, crusty warts on his ankles and calves resembling barnacles. He said nothing. He was utterly immobile. He just looked at Loren impassively, an arrow in his lap. The community stood all around him.

LOREN. Bom dia. Mi nombre es Loren. My name is Loren. Fala Português? No? Okay, I'll speak in English…

You may have seen me. I came over, in a plane. Over the village. We landed on the river. And this man here, with red cheeks – I followed him into your community. I need a guide to take me back to the river.

To the river? The river? Javari. Javari?

ACTOR. It was clear that the name of the river was not that for them. Red Cheeks, who he had pointed to, began to speak urgently, loudly, haranguing the chief.

SFX: voice of Red Cheeks on mini-speaker, moved around the binaural head.

Pointing at Loren, he didn't sound or look particularly welcoming. His voice grew louder. But then others joined in. There was an argument. Everyone was discussing him, pointing at him. Even the children. The headman made no gesture but he looked at Loren and suddenly smiled at him, with teeth like shards of black obsidian. And then as quickly as it had started, the interview was over and people drifted away and Loren was made to advance back along the fallen log to the centre of the village. He was no longer the centre of attention.

SFX: jumble of voices.

The heat was oppressive. He took on water. He was frustrated by his inability to communicate with them. This had never happened to him before. There was no way of getting back to his camp. He was furious with himself for not marking his passage.

LOREN. That was dumb. I should have marked my trail. Well, I'm either in a jam or I'm starting a great experience. But that was the dumbest thing I've done in twenty-five years.

The ACTOR *moves to the desk and puts down the speaker.*

ACTOR. An hour before dusk, he was adopted by a family of four who offered him the use of a hammock in their hut. He stood in the doorway.

During the following, the ACTOR *takes photos of the community. Repeated SFX: camera shutter.*

LOREN. Just beautiful light!

ACTOR. He noticed again that the whole village felt temporary, the huts half-finished. They hadn't even cut a clearing in the forest. They'd just used the space around a fallen tree. Why? Why was that?

LOREN. It's as if they're hiding. And the people look hungry…

God, they're emaciated. Doesn't look like they've eaten in days. What's going on?

ACTOR. Across the village, he could see a girl with strikingly shiny eyes. She was eating beiju, forest bread made from manioc flour.

GIRL. Tuti? Tuti!

ACTOR. The boy he'd followed through the forest suddenly appeared at her side.

LOREN. Tuti. So that is his name. Hey, Tuti?

Takes a photograph. SFX: camera shutter.

Thanks, buddy.

I wonder what I'm starting by photographing these people. I wouldn't want to see them inundated by government agents and anthropologists. They have no defence against infection. I wouldn't want them to become dependent on outsiders; that's the saddest effect of acculturation. The best safeguard is really not to contact them at all.

Hey, buddy!

SFX: camera shutter.

Thanks.

I'm alone though… and I'm only going to be here a few days. My effect on them will be limited…

SFX: camera shutter.

Great shot.

And I hope... unlasting.

ACTOR. He climbed into his hammock, feeling more alone than it is possible to be. Alone in a special sense, because he was in the middle of a busy community. As the light faded, he thought he heard the voice of Red Cheeks, the man he'd followed into the forest, angry, out in the clearing.

He closed his eyes to shut it out, and then he noticed an obscure murmur. A strange inner hum. He realised he'd had this sensation before, when he was standing in front of the headman. The man with barnacles on his legs. Was it coming from the people? Perhaps he was simply imagining it. Perhaps it was just in his unconscious? Or just his response to being alone in their midst. He lay back into his unconscious.

SFX: fragments of recorded interviews.

IAIN McGILCHRIST. *Earlier you talked about your child, and watching this little consciousness grow. And of course the child is not a tabula rasa, it's not a blank sheet. The child comes with certain ways of being, and these are then enormously enriched and made to grow by the intercourse between the baby and those around it, usually the mother and the father, and other members of the family. And what is happening there, is that over a couple of years, the first eighteen months to two years of life, the child is negotiating a very complicated fact, which is that he or she is already a distinct being, and is also interconnected with all the beings around it...*

STEVEN ROSE. *...one of the problems we have is that our consciousness of ourselves, the stories we tell about ourselves and the ways in which we view the world around us are so profoundly social and so profoundly shaped by technology and culture that it's difficult to think outside it.*

MARCUS DU SAUTOY. *...but there's talk now of time actually being an emergent phenomenon...*

GEORGE MARSHALL. *But we're frightened of the future because we don't like the way that the world is going and we feel that. We're also frightened of our own mortality. We're also locked into a kind of short-term consumerism which is about immediate gratification or moving on to the next product.*

REBECCA SPOONER. *…I was very negatively going to say there is no future, but I don't know if I truly believe that…*

5. The Dream

Each sentence below is looped, overlapping with the next, creating a dreamlike effect.

LOREN. One fifth of the world's fresh water is here. The river, four thousand miles long. A thousand miles to the east, the mouth. Connected. Flowing to the ocean. The Arctic. Where does it begin?

ACTOR. Loren McIntyre was flying, suspended, airborne. Hovering above a vision of the jungle and mountains. Like an oversized map. It was a dream and in the dream he knew it. A vast stretch of jungle spread out beneath him and to the east, the two-hundred-mile-wide mouth of the Amazon River, and the ocean flowing all the way to the Arctic. Clouds hanging in the sky, heavy with water vapour. And the source of the Amazon was somewhere in the mountains behind him. The forest; phosphorescent as if lit from underneath. The phosphorescence was the forest's rich life forms, its treasure. The Christian conquistadors were wrong. Pizarro was wrong. Francisco de Orellana was wrong. The oil prospectors, the rubber tappers, the missionaries with their faith had all been wrong. They were all looking for something else, but in his dream McIntyre recognised it instantly, although it didn't have any words.

LOREN. It's the intricacy of the forest… that's the treasure.

ACTOR. Something suffused the greenness of the jungle, all fed by a single source. Hidden somewhere in the mountains. An invisible force; all interconnected, pregnant with a captive message.

LOREN. What is it?

ACTOR. Then suddenly he was sitting in front of the headman, the dream's camera lens focusing first on the man's legs, with their big warts, before lifting to his face.

LOREN. Barnacle.

6. Deeper into the Forest

ACTOR. He was rudely awakened.

SFX: huts coming down, intersperses and overlays the following text.

He stepped out, the post came down, the roof came down, people were gathered in the clearing, arms filled with baskets, drinking gourds, bows and arrows, fishnets. On his right and left, other huts were coming down. Suddenly the headman himself walked along the crowd as if passing it in review. On an unspoken command, the tribe moved off into the forest.

LOREN. Where the hell are they going? Dammit. What is this, where are they going again?

ACTOR. He couldn't stay here alone. He rushed to catch them up.

SFX: breathing, looped.

LOREN. Goddammit.

ACTOR. He was now part of they, walking swiftly along like a Mayoruna whose possessions, instead of being bows and arrows, happened to be a pen, a notebook, and a camera.

SFX: camera shutter.

Half an hour later they crossed a muddy stream. He knew it was half an hour because he kept checking his wristwatch, as though trying to stay in contact with the clock-operated world.

LOREN. Goddammit.

ACTOR. He was being swallowed by the Amazon growth on its own terms. And he knew it. He knew the dangers.

The following from LOREN *is looped to create a jumbled internal monologue.*

LOREN. Fungi. Bacteria. Intestinal parasites. Radical fluctuations in temperature. A lack of cooked food. No purified water.

ACTOR. These things wove their menace around him – a macabre aura, surging up from his unconscious, like a river.

LOREN. Calm down; think of something else. Keep your mind on the pictures. Just think about the *pictures*. (*Looped as a reassurance*.)

Come on, you're gonna get the big one! The superlative shot! That could be the cover of the *Geographic*.

ACTOR. But as he panted behind the headman, he thought, what a ludicrous ambition! Photographers are always so momentary, so fickle. Trying to fix time into one moment. Trying to 'take' a picture. What lay behind this frenzy, Loren thought, was fear. Fear of the future. Fear of losing the past. So unlike these people, he thought. They never think of the future, they don't hoard or store up belongings. Time for them was an invisible companion, something comfortable and unseen like the air. For the civilizados, time was a possession. An increasingly more efficient machine.

SFX: collage of western sounds relating to time.

Late that afternoon, they broke into what had once been the most enormous clearing.

Barnacle stopped, making everyone stop.

SFX: thunder.

A sudden rainstorm lashed down. There was no protection from an upper canopy in this place. Loren thought about the river's ability to rise in an instant, flooding the forest.

7. The First Communication

ACTOR. He watched the community in astonishment.

The ACTOR *uses various sticks to create the sound of huts being constructed, looped on the binaural head. There are sounds all around.*

They were building another settlement. What was the purpose of that? They'd hardly finished building the last one when they had destroyed it and now they were building this one, a little further on. It seemed to accomplish nothing. And again he noticed how starving and exhausted they looked.

In the middle of the clearing, he saw the headman, whom he had now christened Barnacle, sitting in front of a fire on his carved stool. His cheeks were gaunt. His eyes were at half-mast, but he could see from a distance that his hands were moving with precision.

The ACTOR *takes a pencil and scratches along the nib, looped at the binaural head.*

He was whittling an arrow.

McIntyre knew that if he were to need help or protection at some point, he would have to get it from someone of stature. He had an idea. He picked up several long fronds of palm twine, tore them into strips, moved towards Barnacle and stood beside him.

The ACTOR *stands beside the binaural head.*

His fingers moved slowly at first, remembering a long-forgotten trade.

The ACTOR *takes some strands of videotape from the box and rustles them. This is looped, and runs under the next dialogue.*

He started to weave an eighteen-strand belt, trusting a trick he had learnt in the merchant navy. A way of connecting with other men and fighting off boredom at sea. Loren let himself be carried by the dance of the fingers. Barnacle's eyes fluttered in appreciation.

BARNACLE (LOREN *voice-over*). *Some of us are friends.*

ACTOR. Instants later, he remembered how Barnacle had said that some of the Mayoruna were friends. But the headman had not spoken. Or had he? No, he hadn't spoken. Not in English and in fact, not at all.

BARNACLE (LOREN *voice-over*). *Some of us are friends.*

ACTOR. It felt like a message though the headman had not spoken. McIntyre spoke no Mayoruna and none of the Mayoruna spoke English. He looked at the headman, but the headman didn't acknowledge him. He leaned closer to him. He was close enough to hear him breathing.

BARNACLE (LOREN *voice-over*). *Some of us are friends.*

ACTOR. Some of us are friends. Some of us are friends? Was it a reassurance or a warning? The headman was working on. His fingers passed hairs around the tip of the arrow.

The beamed message faded. Maybe being so near to him explained the sensation. His mind then unconsciously adding words in English afterwards.

He had an idea. He strained and applied a focus, not on the words of his next thought, but on the content. Instead of thinking...

LOREN. Hey, buddy, I am a friend too, you can trust me...

ACTOR. ...he tried to fill himself with the feelings of that thought. Then he waited.

BARNACLE (LOREN *voice-over*). *I know.*

ACTOR. ...somehow appeared in his mind. Or maybe it was just the feeling of the answer with his own words, in English, hurrying in to illustrate it.

Suddenly the headman rose and held out a finished arrow. It was a gift, he took it.

When Barnacle was several yards away he reached into his memory. No, he had not spoken out loud and Barnacle understood no English. He strained his ears, remembering yesterday's buzzing, wondering whether he was going insane. He meaninglessly checked his watch as if that single piece of western machinery could counterbalance what he was hearing. It was that unique ambience. There were so many things here in their pure state, why not thought, too? Why not the simplest form of human contact – mind to mind. No, for goodness' sake. But then it had been ratified, because he had been given a gift.

8. Boy and Early Man

SFX: rain.

ACTOR. The rain came again. The adults took shelter in the half-finished huts and the children splashed out to play. His friend Tuti ran across the clearing, laughing, then stopped, panting under some leaves.

SFX: camera shutter.

Raindrops trickled down them in separate sets of three. For a moment Loren put his camera away and just watched the little boy watching the rain.

The ACTOR *creates and loops the pop, pop, pop of the rain dripping from the leaves. Then the sound of feet pounding and the boy singing to himself.*

He started to pound the ground with his little feet. Loren stood and watched. Early man, he thought, had gained the concept of succession, the earliest symbol of the passing of time by observing natural phenomena. Dripping water from faucets, the repeated call of birds, man's own heartbeat. His first clues that time existed in a pulsing vein, invisibly uniting all life. From such early rhythms of nature, dance was born, to stay with man for ever. Loren watched. He watched Tuti dancing the dance of the rain. Devising a game, and an interpretation of reality, from three drops of rain.

The ACTOR *dances. Fragments of sound recordings are heard as they dance.*

MARCUS DU SAUTOY. *And then you see these dots being counted on, and at the end of thirteen dots there's this huge great big animal, above the thirteenth dot, and it's thirteen weeks, thirteen quarters of the moon after the Pleiades emerges is when this happens. To understand time you have to understand something a bit ritualistic, something which is repeating…*

NOMA. *One. Two. Three. Four. Five. Six. Seven. Eight. Nine. Ten…*

The ACTOR *stops dancing and returns to the desk.*

ACTOR. Meanwhile, downriver, men from Loren's world were busy elaborating plans that would deliver Tuti to the world of machinery, and televised news, soft drinks and government welfare.

The ACTOR *picks up a small speaker that begins to play an advertising jingle, moving it around the binaural head.*

Tuti danced on unsuspectingly. Some of us are friends.

Petru recording, played on the ACTOR*'s phone.*

PETRU. *Every time you go and spend time with a tribe like that, you change them to an extent. You bring them over to a stage of civilisation that they would reach perhaps, but you bring them over too fast. On the other hand you, as the scientist, you gain immensely from having been immersed in the experience. So it is our gain, we the modern people, and it is usually their loss. If we decide never to contact tribes any more, then we will never… we will never… find out the deepest, most interesting and controversial things about ourselves. We will not find it out. On the other hand, how will they develop? More slowly, although they have always developed more slowly. They will still get to our civilisation at one time or another. Material progress is unfortunately unavoidable. More coffee?*

ACTOR. A little while later, the fires were restarted and beiju was cooked. And Loren noticed that Barnacle had not eaten. He was back making his whistling arrows. Why hadn't he eaten?

LOREN. He's fasting. Why is he fasting?

ACTOR. *Some of us are friends. (Looped.)*

SFX: door creaking open. The following is a conversation between the ACTOR*, live, and a child, Noma McBurney, recorded aged five.*

NOMA. *Dada, I'm hungry.*

ACTOR. Sweetie, please… You're supposed to be in bed.

NOMA. *Dada, why have you got your shoes on in the house?
You don't want to get the floor dirty.*

ACTOR. Well, I know, but Mama's not here, so…

NOMA. *I'm hungry! Can I have something to eat please?*

ACTOR. There isn't anything. Well, okay, I've got this packet
of crisps. There you go, there's a crisp. Now, I am working…

NOMA. *Night-night, Dada, give me a kiss.*

ACTOR. Now go to bed. And don't slam the door please, I've
got a headache.

SFX: door slamming.

9. Around the Face of Time

ACTOR. What's in these?

*The ACTOR reads some of the ingredients from the back
of the packet and then crunches a few crisps. The bag
rustles. The sound is looped and turns into the crackle of
a burning fire.*

He woke feeling fingers on his left wrist. He felt up with his
right. His watch was gone. He looked up. And saw faces
looking down at him… A nauseating smell of burning rubber
and smoke filled his nostrils… He looked over the side of his
hammock and he realised what it was.

LOREN. My Adidas trainers. They're burning them; they're
burning my shoes.

ACTOR. He swung out of his hammock and pushed his way
through the group of people out into the plaza. There was a
fire. His shoes were melting, on the flames. His watch was
already a black disc.

LOREN. Hey, fellas! I need those. Those are my Adidas trainers. You don't need them I do.

The ACTOR *slips into them and reacts violently, as if the soles of their feet were scalded.*

Okay, you've burnt my shoes. You've killed my watch. At least I've still got my camera.

SFX: camera shutter.

My camera! I'd fallen asleep with it on my hip and now I didn't have it.

I rushed back to my hut and searched my hammock. No camera anywhere. I pushed back out into the plaza. My heart was racing in front of me. The community were all gathered, looking at me. I wanted to seize them, shout, where is my camera? Give me my camera! Calm down. They're naked, they can't hide a black box anywhere.

I saw Red Cheeks watching me, his arms folded. When I caught his eye, he turned away. Calm down, calm down. Across the plaza I saw Barnacle arriving. He seemed innocent in all this, looking to right and left at his people to see what was going on. They avoided his eyes and started to drift away. Then I realised they had been trying to hex me. Burning personal belongings is almost always a hex. I knew I had to act. I had to do something before the moment passed. I was being ostracised. I had to get their attention. I had no idea what I should do... so I did the first thing that came into my head.

The ACTOR *goes to a multi-pack of water, removes the packaging and uses the packaging to create a loop of scrunching around the binaural head. They breathe heavily with each movement, then begin to run, still using the packets to create the sound of feet on leaves.*

SFX: looped version of the above.

I started jogging around the perimeter of the village.

I watched my feet pound the grass. One lap. Two laps. Three laps. I heard my own thoughts projected right back at me in panic. Calm down. But running felt good, liberating.

I passed Red Cheeks, screaming something at his friends. They had hexed me, now I was hexing them, casting a spell of my own. Now they were starting to watch, they were all coming back. Barnacle was scanning his crowd, trying to interpret their reactions. Whenever I passed him, I exploded into a hammering of fists and feet, almost a parody of intent.

LOREN (*pre-record*). *I can't think of anything else to do. I've got to get through to you.*

LOREN. Five laps.

LOREN (*pre-record*). *We have to communicate. We are communicating.*

LOREN. Ten laps.

LOREN (*pre-record*). *I want to survive. I want you to survive as well.*

LOREN. I ran on. Fifteen, twenty laps. I slowed down, walked a lap. Stopped in front of Barnacle. Dripping with sweat. What was he going to do? Then he turned and started jogging. Just the way I had gone.

SFX: loop plays in reverse as the ACTOR *stands, watching the track of Barnacle running.*

Following my tracks. But in the opposite direction. Counterclockwise. He was undoing my spell. And as he passed me, he beat his fists and feet as I had done.

BARNACLE (LOREN *voice-over*). *I don't know if this will work. I don't know if my people will follow me.*

LOREN. Was I losing my mind?

BARNACLE (LOREN *voice-over*). *I have no alternative… I have to try to make it work.*

LOREN. I felt I was inside his head, literally thinking his thoughts.

I'm not psychic; I don't believe in that shit… Still I received it.

BARNACLE (LOREN *voice-over*). *Other white people have been before. They brought death. My people are dying now to avoid that death.*

LOREN. This was some bigger emergency – a threshold of some kind in the tribe's life…

Barnacle ran until his chest became a mirror of sweat. He ran at the limit of his strength, and he was fasting, remember. His people now began to utter cries of encouragement, as if wanting to instil him with energy… Red Cheeks had drifted off, disgusted. Barnacle ran on but now, his messages no longer glowed in my mind, but had dissolved into a residual beaming, a sort of leftover. It crystallised into this.

BARNACLE (LOREN *voice-over*). *The face of time.*

LOREN. The face of time? Eighteen, nineteen, twenty laps.

He slowed to a walk and everyone hailed their chief. Barnacle stopped in front of me. He raised a finger and said something solemn. I looked at the space he and I had circled, performing our competing spells. What was that in my head? Did he really say that? The face of time.

I slipped my feet into the remains of my chargrilled Adidas trainers… I looked into the forest, trying to calm myself down. I looked up at a black creeper… Fuck! That's not a creeper, that's my film. A black strip of film, hanging from a branch. Fuck! I've been running with two rolls of exposed film in my pockets. Only one roll of film left. Those are my shots! Who put that there? And then I looked a little higher up the tree and I saw my camera. In the hands of a woolly monkey. A woolly monkey clutching my camera… It must have been a pet of one of the kids.

'Hey… Hey!' He climbed higher. 'For god's sake, don't open it!' What was I doing, I was talking to a monkey? I threw a stick. He caught it. Bad idea. He was poking with it at the camera. The back flew open. He ripped out the film. The spool popped out. And he ripped the camera apart in one movement.

SFX: camera is ripped apart. A jumble of voices. The words 'The. Great. Shot.' are heard.

ACTOR. Loren McIntyre's knees gave way and he just sank to the floor. He sat there. Inches from his damaged camera. Useless. Reduced. Reduced to one roll of film. How could he prove that he had been there? What was he going to give *National Geographic*? He was reduced to just a body.

Purposeless. He was a tourist now. No watch. He would have to live by nature's clock. He would have to be like these people.

Petru recording, played on the ACTOR*'s phone.*

PETRU. *After this, Barnacle, as is described in the book, became extremely friendly, and he started to spend time with him. And to sort of protect – anyway, Barnacle and McIntyre, became a sort of inseparable item.*

10. What Was in the Dark

LOREN. Barnacle indicated that we should walk into the forest together. We passed children gathered round a shaman. They were looking at caterpillars, insects, plants. I imagined he was showing them the law of the forest. Pretty soon they'll be able to survive on their own in the forest.

Once we were alone, the communication started again. Smooth and implicit. And even though he was a few yards away, he communicated to me that:

You are sad because what was in the dark should have stayed in the dark.

It was so clear, I couldn't believe he hadn't spoken. Was he talking about my camera? No, how could he be? But it was so much like speaking… for a moment, I couldn't accept it and I shouted:

'Fala Português?'

He leaked into my mind somehow that he didn't understand my words. I went and stood quite close to him. I had to accept what was happening, or else I had to assume I was hallucinating. Barnacle communicated something like:

Here's the forest; if you run away right now, I'm not going to stop you.

I said nothing. Again he said:

Other white people have been here. They brought death.

It is almost impossible to describe the exact nature of the communication between us. The clearest description I can give is that it was like a kind of dialogue. He said:

BARNACLE (LOREN *voice-over*). *We have been moving around.*

LOREN. I tried to communicate back: have you been attacked?

BARNACLE (LOREN *voice-over*). *Yes. By white people that came down from the sky.*

LOREN. So where are you moving to?

BARNACLE (LOREN *voice-over*). *We're going to the beginning?*

LOREN. What beginning?

BARNACLE (LOREN *voice-over*). *The beginning.*

LOREN. We walked back to the village. Barnacle scanned me with his eyes. What they spelled was clear, no beaming necessary: what was I going to do? I was asking myself the same question. What am I going to do? *What am I going to do?* (*Looped.*)

Petru recording, played on the ACTOR*'s phone.*

PETRU. *But he kept telling us, 'How can I say this – the* Geographic *is going to jump on me?' I said, Loren, no one is going to jump on you. You may create some controversy, regarding whether you believe that what happened happened, but that's not like, it's not a case for fraud or anything…*

IRIS. *…I would say that, we got him comfortable though…*

PETRU. *…We got him comfortable, and, he was towards the age, to which he wanted to talk about it.*

ACTOR. He was towards the age at which he wanted to talk about it.

SFX: collage of voices from the ACTOR*'s unconscious.*

NOMA. *Can you know what I'm thinking, inside my head?*

STEVEN ROSE. *Of course you need your brain, I need my brain to think, I need my brain to be conscious. But that doesn't mean that consciousness is in my brain, any more than the fact that I need my legs to walk means that it's my legs that are doing the walking.*

IAIN McGILCHRIST. *Everything in the world is only known in comparison to everything else that we know. There isn't a way of getting out of this. The myth that we're up against nowadays is that there is some abstract, objective reality that is beyond our myth-making, beyond our language, beyond metaphor, which is absolute rather than relative. But there is no such thing.*

11. The Night Hunt

The ACTOR *returns to the desk and loops breathing into the microphone.*

LOREN. I slept until I thought I was dreaming of a jaguar and its grunt. And then I woke. There was a jaguar. In the village. A jaguar in the village. I sat bolt upright. In the nearest hut, children cried in panic, the noise of the village tripled in volume.

I heard Red Cheeks screaming. Six or seven other young men brandishing spears and burning branches, ganged up in the middle of the clearing. I found myself in front of the gang of young men and Red Cheeks gestured for me to follow him. I'd always wanted to see a jaguar hunt so I stepped closer to him. But I was furious with myself for not having my camera.

SFX: jaguar grunt.

We scrambled over the wet grass into a solid wall of fogged-up forest vegetation. The torches went away into the darkness like flares. Keep up, come on. I'm in my mid-fifties, they're in their twenties. The worst scenario would be to be left alone in the dark. The grunt rang out again.

SFX: jaguar grunt.

Where are they?

AYYYAYYA!

I heard Red Cheeks shout unexpectedly. The young men had stopped right in front of a spiny thickness. The beast had crawled underneath it – a cluster of thorny plants between the roots of a huge tree. I headed for it as fast as I could so as not to miss the spectacle. Red Cheeks suddenly pushed me. Powered by this and my own momentum, I ran straight into the thornbush.

He dropped his torch and stepped on it. The other burning branches disappeared in the same instant.

Total dark followed.

I was trapped.

Darkness. Sound of the thornbush created live using brushes on the ears of the binaural head.

I thought of the jaguar, and then I realised there wasn't one. Red Cheeks had imitated the grunt himself and now I'm alone. The jungle is all around me. Where are they? Listen. They've gone back to the village. I've got to get out of the thornbush. The thorns are in my arms, my legs, my body. I could die ten times over before anybody finds me. Come on. Get out of this, just push out. It doesn't matter how painful it is, just push out.

I try to pluck the barbs out of my skin. I can't get them out. I wave my arms in the air to coagulate the bleeding... The sound of insects begins to grow, louder and fuller.

SFX: mosquitos and flies all around the binaural head.

I'm like a magnet.

Formations and formations of gnats streak through the air towards me. I scratch an arm; they pucker my face. I've got to move, to shake them off. I creep away slowly. A creeper hits me in the face, then another. I tell myself, okay, an animal would sense my approach. Less gnats. I breathe. I stop. They find me again. I dance. This is a torture. I have to think about something else.

Think of something else. Think of evolution. I can't see anything and then I do see something. A spider. Whose four pairs of eyes are luminous. I bring my eyes so close to him that his eyes are probably reflected in mine.

I edge closer. Through the eyes, I look into a palpitating mass of electric fire, the light is coming from within. How did he evolve this way? How did Barnacle evolve to talk to me this way? Time. Time is the answer.

A snake slithers along the branch, towards the spider. He cries some sort of distress on the spider frequency, the snake gobbles him up and then we are back in darkness.

Total darkness.

12. Lost in the Forest

LOREN. I wake up, scratching. The bugs have found me again, laid their eggs in the open cuts left by the thorns. Feels like screwworms.

There's light. I immediately move, to try to find the village. I work my way back. Good – a trail! I feel saved. But then I find another, diverging. The thrill of finding the first trail withers instantly.

Either one could lead to life or death. Death is already here. It's always here in the wilderness.

I've got to walk. I can't afford to stop for fear the tribe might move out of range. Choose one, choose one!

BARNACLE (LOREN *voice-over*). *We're going to the beginning.*

What was that he said? They're going to the beginning. They're going to move, you've got to move. But try not to move in a circle. I have to move as fast as possible and hope for some luck.

A light ahead. Humidity. Higher temperature. The canopy is punctured and sunlight pours into a clearing. I step in.

The clearing is littered with hacked-off branches. Technological man was here!

SFX: jumble of voices, the sound of a chainsaw and drilling.

REBECCA SPOONER. *And because of the price of oil these very remote regions are being opened up to that kind of very expensive work. Which before wouldn't have been economically viable. But now, because the oil is worth so much, companies are going into very remote Amazon areas and looking for oil…*

MILTON FRIEDMAN. *Is there some society you know that doesn't run on greed?*

JESS WORTH. *They're all over the world. They're in Latin America, they're in North America, they've recently gone into tar sands, which is probably the most destructive source of fossil fuels in the world, they've gone heavily into Russia, where they're trying to drill in the Russian Arctic, they're here in the UK, they're drilling in the North Sea, they're in Australia, they're trying to drill in ultra-deep water, deeper than deep-water horizon, which created this catastrophic spill in the gulf of Mexico…*

LOREN. Hello!!

Is anybody there?

I'm close to my fellow modern man. The rapacious developer, as objectionable as he may be, I welcome his presence… They can't be far.

Hello! Is anybody here?

I see a thick rope on the floor, a cable, and then I realise it's not a cable, but a traffic of army ants. I follow the procession away from the anthill and find… a watch. I look at it. And then I understand and before I can fully articulate the thought, I start running along the freeway of ants and I find… four bodies.

BARNACLE (LOREN *voice-over*). *Other white people have been before, they brought death.*

LOREN. They're piled on top of each other. A baseball cap, jaws without gums, teeth stained by tobacco. And they seem in some sort of motion, as the ants crawl over them.

I notice an arrow coming out of the hulk of a chest, and then I see another one lying on the ground, loosened out of flesh.

Should I wait here? Will there be a rescue? It seems silly to think so...

Somewhere in this mess there might be wallets with the names of these people, but I can't bring myself to grope around inside of what's left of them with my hands.

Calm down, calm down.

I notice a swelling on my left arm. With my knife I cut it open and pull out a white maggot. I remember its scientific name, Callitroga Hominivorax. Hominivorax means devourer of man – an infestation can kill in a week. I keep walking.

Where is the river?

Where is the river? I have to keep moving. I walk for an hour. One-fifth of the world's fresh water is here in the Amazon basin but I can't find any water. The heat is overbearing, every twenty minutes or so I break a segment from a vine, like an extra-long cucumber, squeeze the juice and drink.

During the following, the ACTOR *drinks and discards several small bottles of water.*

It has a bitter taste. I don't think it's toxic but it's got more liquid than other vines. I suck on thirty of these because I need to and then I find I reach an interesting state of inebriation.

The forest becomes my brain and my brain the forest. I have the sensation of seeing my thoughts.

SFX: jumble of words.

DAVID FARMER. *A recognition that we are actually part of nature, and that the whole system is interacting and that our future, our life, is...*

LOREN. I keep moving and the slight hallucination changes. But I feel that my hand groping around the universe has torn a corner open. Soon there will be an encounter. I panic, why did I tear that corner open? I'm not prepared for this encounter; it's true. I'm not prepared. Not like the spider swallowed by the snake. And then a thought suddenly howls, savagely.

I was never part of nature.

No, I'm not!!

DAVID FARMER. …*a recognition that we are actually part of nature…*

LOREN. No I'm not. None of us were. We're human beings. We're not part of nature.

DAVID FARMER. … *we are actually part of nature, and we cannot escape from it, just as we cannot escape from the planet.*

The ACTOR *pulls themself up to the table.*

LOREN. I jackknife and fall on my stomach on rotting leaves. I order myself to crawl but my body refuses to obey and I remain lying, thinking of what will happen to me if I lose consciousness. Which animal's going to eat me first? It'll be the forest pigs, they eat everything.

I manage to raise my face through sheer force of will, and I see a lion marmoset, the smallest of all primates, observing me from a palm frond with a little humid look in his eye, as if ready to burst into tears. But I know he won't weep. Only man weeps. My last conscious impression is the marmoset's eyes.

Death is a bank of lights being switched off, a vast theatre in my head, it grows like a cacophony, dims, and then black.

SFX cut: blackout, silence.

Then…

NOMA. *Twinkle twinkle little star*
How I wonder what you are
Like a diamond in the sky
Twinkle twinkle little star
How I wonder what you are.

13. Burning the Past

The ACTOR *hums, loops the sound, and creates layers of chanting.*

ACTOR. The Mayoruna found him, yards from the river, and bought him back to the village.

For five days, he sweated with high fever in a hammock, under the hands of two shamen who pulled gently at his limbs. They turned him over and sucked the maggots and thorns from his back. And the demons from his forehead. They stood either side of his hammock, chanting, chanting. He slept, woke, slept again, woke again.

At one point he thought he saw a face in the doorway of the hut.

LOREN. *Barnacle.* (*Looped.*)

ACTOR. Drifting between dream and reality. When he finally awoke and the fever was gone, it was morning and he was alone.

He swung out of his hammock and staggered tentatively out of the hut and into the plaza. The community seemed to be waiting. Their cheeks seemed pulled downwards by an invisible weight. Mouths stubbornly shut. Thinner. Weary. What were they waiting for?

He stumbled past an open doorway, glanced in and stopped as if electrocuted.

LOREN. Red Cheeks.

ACTOR. What Loren saw was a body sewn inside a funeral basket.

Red Cheeks' face could be glimpsed inside, convulsed. His head seemed to be smouldering, but when Loren looked closer, the smoke was just the movement of bugs, swarming round his head.

He turned and across the plaza, he saw Barnacle. Watching him as if making sure he witnessed all of this.

LOREN. He saved my life. Why?

ACTOR. Barnacle's gaze didn't waver.

LOREN. I wanted to resist him, but something came into my mind…

BARNACLE (LOREN *voice-over*). *They were holding us still, still in time*.

LOREN. They were holding us still, still in time? What does he mean? Oh I see, it's a political thing. He's put down an insurrection.

BARNACLE (LOREN *voice-over*). *When they burn up, we move away*.

LOREN. When they burn up we move away? What does he mean?

Soon after that they set the huts on fire. Everything burned. They moved off into the forest again.

Exhausted breathing, looped.

Red Cheeks' body is going up in flames now. We walk. What's happening? Where are we going? I strain my ears, hoping against hope for the sound of a plane. I hear nothing. We walk all that day. We stop at sundown. No evening meal. We sleep on the forest floor. Nothing to eat the next morning. It's the same the next day and the next day and the next day… I'm walking close behind Barnacle.

I'm going to beam something. Where are we going? I ask him.

BARNACLE (LOREN *voice-over*). *To the beginning*.

LOREN. The beginning?

BARNACLE (LOREN *voice-over*). *The beginning*.

LOREN. And what are we going to find in your goddamn beginning?

I stop. And then suddenly I realised that his answer might be 'death'. Death is awaiting us in the beginning.

I look at the people… I'm searching for signs of resistance in their eyes, but they drift past me, as if I am invisible. Day four. Day five. The older people are limping. Women break off branches, grabbing fruit to feed the children, who loll vacant-eyed over their parents' shoulders. This is madness.

We drink water incessantly. I'm going to take leave of
Barnacle and his people. I'll follow them to the first
navigable body of water, use a log as a raft… I'll take my
chances. I'll take my chances.

14. Cambio

LOREN. Days pass. And then, I recognise a human scent,
smoke or cooked meat or decomposition. What is it?

Oh my god, a village! A settlement! Maybe they have a
plane, or a boat, or a radio?

And suddenly a crowd of tribespeople storms forward
through the trees.

Mayoruna – but less gaunt, less emaciated. They rush to
surround the newcomers, the children, touching, jumping,
the adults smiling and exchanging loud greetings.

Barnacle disappears in a circle of women and youngsters –
his family. I see Tuti, throwing himself on the old man,
hugging him. Barnacle swings the boy up onto his shoulders.
Why had I never guessed he was Barnacle's son?

And suddenly we're eating.

SFX: the ACTOR *eating, looped.*

Gobbling, gorging. I feel drunk with food, drunk with
momentary survival.

And then – (*The* ACTOR *looks towards the binaural head.*)
amongst these new people, I see a man, a shaman with a
conical hat, looking at me. He's wearing shorts. A pair of
tattered shorts. He's wearing shorts. I hold my breath. I step
closer to him and I say:

The ACTOR *turns the binaural head to face them.*

Olá. Meu nome é Loren.

Fala Português?

The following dialogue is spoken live by the ACTOR, *switching between a pitched-up microphone for* CAMBIO, *and pitched-down microphone for* LOREN.

Music.

I turn away in bitter disappointment. I'm walking away, when over my shoulder, I hear...

CAMBIO. Lowen, sim. Bem-vindo, Lowen, cambio.

LOREN. He's speaking to me in Portuguese. He says, 'Welcome, Loren.' And then again, immediately 'Cambio.' Cambio means 'over', in radio parlance. He just greeted me with 'Welcome, Loren, over.' I'm about to hug him. I have so many things to say. Listen, I don't know how long I've been with these people... I've lost count of days... I had a watch but... I'm waiting for a plane... There's too much. Just ask something simple.

Is this your village? Está é sua aldeia?

CAMBIO. Sim, minha aldeia, cambio.

LOREN. 'Yes, my village, over.'

So these people are relatives of yours? Então essas pessoas são sua família?

CAMBIO. Meu povo, cambio.

LOREN. 'My people, over.'

How come you speak Portuguese?

Como que você fala Português?

From here on, the voice of Cambio is pre-recorded with voice modification. The Portuguese and the English translation are therefore fluid and overlapping.

CAMBIO. *Seis anos atrás, homens armados, trabalhando para construtores, atacaram a gente. Mas eu consegui fugi. Encontrei um lugar seguro, uma missão. Eu consegui um trabalho com empregado para um operador de rádio e lá aprendi, cambio.*

LOREN. 'Six years ago, gunmen came, working for developers. They attacked us but I got away. I found a place of safety in a mission. I got work for the radio operator and I learned, over.'

What's your name?

Qual é o seu nome?

CAMBIO. *Eles me chamaram Cambio. Cambio.*

LOREN. 'They call me Over. Over.'

SFX: fire.

Smoke hits my eyes. A vast fire has been lit and both communities are gathered round the flames. They carry their belongings and pile them next to the fire. Axes, manioc graters, calabashes, fishhooks, personal belongings. Another great mound of objects is forming. Painstakingly crafted objects, critical for the tribe's survival, things they would never mindlessly abandon.

Barnacle watches, Tuti upon his shoulders.

What's this, Cambio? O que é isso, Cambio?

CAMBIO. *A cerimônia, cambio.*

LOREN. 'The ceremony, over.'

For what?

CAMBIO. *Estamos retornando.*

LOREN. 'We're returning,' he says.

CAMBIO. *Essas coisas morrem aqui, para podermos retornar.*

LOREN. 'These things die here, so we can return.'

What do you mean? You're going back in time?

CAMBIO. *Não, não voltando no tempo. Retornando. Como… uma passagem de volta, cambio.*

LOREN. 'No, not going back. Returning. Like… return ticket, over.'

So let me get this straight, you're going to destroy everything the tribe needs?

CAMBIO. *Os espíritos deles estão impedindo a gente de voltar. Eles estão com ciúmes.*

LOREN. 'Their spirits are stopping us, over. They are jealous.'

CAMBIO. *Eles seguram a gente no tempo. Cambio.*

LOREN. 'They hold us still. Still in time. Over.'

Just as Barnacle had said, the same words.

Listen, Cambio… I don't speak Mayoruna but the headman of this tribe, with the boy on his shoulders, he told me about your return to the beginning…

Cambio looked shocked. He cleared his throat.

CAMBIO. *Talvez ele te falou na outra língua, a língua velha, cambio.*

LOREN. 'Maybe he spoke to you in the other language, the old language, over.'

No, no, I think he talked to me without words.

CAMBIO. *Sim, essa é a outra língua, a antiga, cambio.*

LOREN. 'Yes. That's the other language, the old language, over.'

What do you mean, the old language? Does it come from another time? How do they learn it?

CAMBIO. *Não, eles nunca aprenderam. Eles simplesmente lembrem, cambio.*

LOREN. 'No, they never learned it. The old ones simply remember, over.'

I feel Barnacle's gaze upon me. I look to where he stands. He takes in his hands the most beautiful arrow, the one he gave me. He wants me to witness all of this. He snaps it in two. This action signals a frenzy of destruction, the tribe breaking, crushing the piled-up objects under their feet. What they can't break with their hands, they crush with their feet. They grind the pots into pieces, crack the trophy skulls, snap the bows and arrows. They shatter the whole pile into bits of wood and bone, feather, husks and loose human teeth strung on necklaces. Everything that was beautiful and useful. Onto the fire, without hesitation or a look of regret.

CAMBIO. *Estamos afrouxando os nossos laços. Ficando mais livre e mais livre. Vela no tempo, cambio.*

LOREN. 'We are loosening our bonds. Getting freer and freer. Sailing in time, over.'

And what will happen when the tribe arrive at their destination? And where will you be then?

CAMBIO. *A merda com tudo isso, cambio.*

LOREN. 'To hell with all this, over.'

I stare at the fire and I imagine us in the west, burning our possessions so as not to remain still in time!

I picture bonfires, like this one, along some affluent American street. People dragging out their paid-for belongings; furniture, appliances, toys. Dragged out. Sprayed with gasoline, bursting in flames. All of a culture, the most materialistic and leisure-minded in the world, up in flames. I saw flames spring up in a front yard, and another, and another. All along the street, all through the neighbourhood and the next and the next.

The sound of the fire is roaring. Music.

Washington. Pennsylvania Avenue, the White House, on fire. The Library of Congress, on fire! Freeing itself, taking off, soaring, carried by the vehicle of the sacrificial, purifying flames. Carried where? Carried where? Doesn't matter! Burning the past! Burning it all. Maybe I'll live to find the answer.

During the following, the ACTOR *exhorts the audience to get rid of the past. The* ACTOR *tries to destroy the plastic bottles, but they won't break. They smash a glass water bottle to pieces, try to destroy the speakers, the endless box of tape, the work desk: they grab a hammer and manically destroy the desk. A frenzy of destruction builds to a climax.*

ACTOR. Come on! Burning the past. This is the past! Let's destroy it, let's burn it all up! Can we destroy this? Fucking plastic... Let's smash this. Get rid of the past. The whole fucking thing. Fuck it...

And then the ACTOR *sees their phone. They hold it out to the audience.*

Okay, the big one… let's get rid of this. That's got all the fucking past in it.

The ACTOR *places it on the broken desk and lifts the hammer.*

SFX: ring.

The following voices are a recording from the past. Onstage, the ACTOR *remains, hammer in hand, staring at the phone on the desk. They are poised to hit it, but never do.*

Hello?

NOMA. *Dada, I had a bad dream.*

ACTOR. *Listen, go back to bed, sweetie.*

NOMA. *Dada, why are you always speaking on your phone?*

ACTOR. *I'm just working, sweetie.*

NOMA. *It's so boring.*

ACTOR. *I know. I'm just working. Who is this? They've hung up.*

NOMA. *Can I play on your phone then?*

ACTOR. *Well, I'm not playing, sweetie. Now, do you want some water?*

NOMA. *No, fizzy water!*

ACTOR. *Well, we don't have any fizzy water, come on, let's get some from the tap.*

NOMA. *Thank you.*

ACTOR. *There you are. Drink it up.*

NOMA. *How long has I been asleep?*

ACTOR. *Oh my sweetie, I don't know, maybe half an hour or something. But you've got to go to sleep now.*

Noma drinks the water, breathing heavily. She breathes deeper and deeper. It modifies and slows, distorts.

15. The Ritual

The voice of Cambio is pre-recorded. The ACTOR *speaks live.*

CAMBIO. *Lowen. Lowen. Vem, Lowen, cambio.*

LOREN. I wake up. I open my eyes and see Cambio's face.

CAMBIO. *Agora, Lowen. Cambio.*

LOREN. 'Now, Loren. Over.'

> What do you mean? I've only been asleep two minutes. We were just in Barnacle's hut. We'd been in there for hours. I swing out of my hammock. It's cold.

> Cambio! What's happening?

CAMBIO. *O começo, cambio.*

LOREN. 'The beginning, Loren, over.'

> Wait. We've just been discussing this in Barnacle's hut. This thing isn't supposed to happen for days yet. And if it does happen now, what if there is nothing at the beginning? What if the old one is crazy? What if we're all going to die?

> Cambio is silent. He looks away, then says: 'No. No, there is no other way out. The old belief has to be proven true.'

CAMBIO. *Agora, Lowen. Cambio.*

LOREN. 'Now, Loren. Over.'

> He pulls me by the arm. The clearing is full of tribesmen. Each wears his cat whiskers.

CAMBIO. *Agora, Lowen. Cambio.*

LOREN. The community are forming a long line, which stretches across the village. They've painted their bodies with black genipap paint. I know what it means. It's begun.

> *The* ACTOR *dances. They create the rhythm again and again, and the pattern builds and loops until a whole village of men can be heard.*

> We watch them. They're beginning to dance.

> One step to the left. Three small. Two to the right and two more back, then back to the start and everyone claps his

hands once, hard. Cambio takes me by the arm. We throw ourselves in.

LOREN *dances*.

We repeat, repeat and repeat and repeat. It's hypnotic. My mind starts to travel over the last three weeks, four weeks? How long?

Music.

SFX: Loren's journey. Fragments of text are heard:

Where's the village? If this is the area where you saw the village…

SFX: plane overhead.

PETRU. *He was towards the age…*

BARNACLE (LOREN *voice-over*). *They were holding us still…*

During the fragments of LOREN*'s journey, the* ACTOR *moves out of the line of dancing men and into the hut.*

LOREN. Suddenly I'm in Barnacle's hut the previous evening. It's filled with men, sitting, smoking green cigars. He invites me to sit. Finally I can talk to him. Cambio can translate.

The ACTOR *delivers the following text, but alongside it and overlapping with it, we hear Barnacle, speaking to* LOREN *in Mayoruna.*

We just look at each other. And through Cambio, he asks:

'You have come here. Why?'

There's silence.

Cambio translates and I say: 'I heard about your people. I wanted to photograph your tribe, to show others that you exist.'

He replies: 'Why have you not left us? Why have you not fled?'

I choose my words carefully. I say: 'I want to see… I want to witness your beginning.'

And then a thought is planted in my mind; Barnacle beams to me that my staying makes the ritual good.

And then he speaks again, through Cambio, and tells me that the tribe in all its forms has been moving for some time. This ritual, he tells me, will bring one life to an end and begin another. What does he mean? I panic.

'Cambio, tell him, there's another way. There's enough space in the forest, there's enough wilderness, nobody's ever going to find you here. I can speak to the Brazilian government, to FUNAI.'

Cambio translates and Barnacle looks at me. He replies: 'No, there is no other way. They will come. They will always come, looking for their oil, with planes and guns and alcohol.'

'So, when will we be in the beginning?' I ask.

'Haven't you noticed?' he replies. 'Time is already falling off.'

'What if we were to hear a plane, right now?'

'We won't.'

And I realise I can't remember the last time I did hear a plane, or see the vapour trails in the sky. I ask: 'Are we close?'

'Very close. You can already feel the signs. And you will see more.'

He passes me a cigar and I drag deeply on it. Barnacle and the other men continue to talk about the beginning, having a philosophical discussion of time, on which they don't seem to agree.

The ACTOR *begins to slowly be drawn towards the dancing.*

I close my eyes. There is a feeling inside me.

'Why am I here?' I ask Barnacle this without words. 'Why am I here?'

And then a thought blooms in my mind, and words cluster to it...

BARNACLE (LOREN *voice-over*). *You will prove that it is real.*

LOREN. Is that why I'm here? You will prove that it is real...

The ACTOR *is dancing. The sound of dancing, pounding feet rises. The sound of voices chanting.*

The heat is overbearing. We are here, thudding with our feet, like a giant hand knocking on a door. The door to the beginning. We shall step through that door.

The drums and pounding feet rise with the claps, and shadows of dancing men fill the floor.

As the ACTOR *dances, we hear voices from recorded interviews, mixed with the live dancing and dialogue.*

REBECCA SPOONER. *The Mayoruna describe the oil underneath the ground as the blood of the earth and they're concerned, like many other indigenous people, that if you suck out that blood, the oil, the life source, then the earth will cease to exist.*

LOREN. We dance all night.

IAIN McGILCHRIST. *Earlier you talked about your child. And watching this little consciousness grow...*

JESS WORTH. *They're in Latin America, they're in North America, they've recently gone into tar sands, which is probably the most destructive source of fossil fuels in the world...*

LOREN. The sun explodes above the horizon. A cycle has ended; another is beginning. Two thousand miles away to the east it is already midday, but here it is morning. A morning loaded with events as yet un-happened. One of those events might be our death.

SFX and music all stop dead. Silence.

We stop. Our bodies cry with exhaustion.

Barnacle appears, a diadem of egret feathers on his head. He passes down the file of men, asking a standard question, to which each man responds.

I need a drink. What's happening?

The sound of Barnacle naming the tribe runs alongside the ACTOR*'s live text.*

BARNACLE. *Kiatoo. Axi. Sava.*

LOREN. They're getting new names, they're choosing new names for the beginning.

BARNACLE. *Ekke. Nutushi. Upopai.*

LOREN. There's a bowl of masato beer being passed around. I haven't drunk all night. I take a huge gulp. It tastes of herbs.

The ACTOR *grabs a large bottle of water and gulps throughout the following.*

Here it comes again. I drink some more.

Barnacle repeats the names seriously, and with a thumb so red it looks bloodied, he puts a print of red urucu on each forehead he passes.

Give me that. I need it. I'm going to hold on to this beer.

Barnacle stops before Cambio. 'Cambio', my friend christens himself. And he winks at me. I don't want to lose my name, even if it is just a memory. I wet my lips and mutter 'McIntyre.'

BARNACLE. *Mackin-tayah. Tayah, aha.*

LOREN. The bright-red thumb stamps my forehead. And the chief steps past me.

As he passes I start to drink, desperately. That's better. I hope there's no drug in that drink.

There is.

I feel a numbing of my limbs. It feels like my bones are liquefying, a liquefaction suggesting a kind of birth. Very slowly, from skeleton hard, they're growing mellower, and sort of coming alive. The air seems to separate into tiny, flexible rivulets of oxygen. I take the bowl as it passes and gulp again. I feel like I could expand and contract distances at will.

I try to stop thinking, try to open myself completely to the present moment. Then I feel like there's two of me. I get a taste of something… I'm now in triplicate… I get an awareness that's frighteningly immediate and overfilled with sensorial stimuli. I try not to censor it, but I tense up as I'm trying and it vanishes.

16. The Frog Ceremony

Through the following, Cambio's voice is pre-recorded and the ACTOR *is live, speaking as* LOREN.

LOREN. Cambio motions me to follow him behind the huts. A mighty croaking of frogs. A group of shamen are reaching with leaves to touch the frogs and spoon off their backs a teary semi-transparent secretion, which they collect, drop by drop, in wooden bowls.

Cambio pulls a frog out, shoots out his tongue, and licks it.

CAMBIO. *Para ver o começo, cambio.*

LOREN. 'To see the beginning, over.'

See the beginning?

CAMBIO. *Ver os animais lá dentro. E conversar com eles. Ver as onças e conversar com elas. Cambio.*

LOREN. 'See the animals in it. Talk to them. See the jaguars and talk to them. Over.'

That's interesting. Okay.

Men sip from the wooden bowls, others hold frogs and put their mouths directly on those bumps and pimples, which keep weeping quietly, like so many ulcers.

One of the shamen raises a knife of chonta palm, like this...

The ACTOR *finds a shard of the broken bottle glass on the floor.*

...and I think he's going to cut open a frog. I turn away but when I turn back, it's not the frog he's cutting. He has sliced open his own forearm. What's he doing?

The ACTOR *takes the glass shard and draws it down their arm. Blood gushes out.*

He's opening it, and he's pouring the frog secretion, straight into the bloodstream. They're going to see the animals now.

I turn around and see Cambio, his forehead has pearled up with sweat. He says 'plants grow inside me' with such conviction that I expect tangles of creepers to push out through his skin. He keels over, sprawls on the ground.

Hey, are you alright, buddy?

Now they're seeing the animals. The clearing is full of cawing, barking, growling men. And although I haven't taken any of the drug I feel like I'm turning into an animal…

The ACTOR*'s voice is modified so low that they begin to sound like an animal. They bark, growl, roar. The modification suddenly sweeps very high, turning them into a bird, shrill, cawing.*

In front of me, a man imitates a macaw so convincingly that his cat tattoos seem in total contradiction to his voice. He invites me to look into his eyes. The tunnels in his pupils are a dark passage into something I'll never visit. So I turn away. I close my eyes. I try to visualise my own version of the beginning.

But I meet no fabulous beasts. I see man.

Labouring across a fogged-up landscape, and I realise that this landscape is not territory, it's time.

I see time. Our time.

SFX montage: fragments of voices overlapping, the sound of drilling and chainsaws.

MILTON FRIEDMAN. *Is there some society you know that doesn't run on greed?*

JESS WORTH. *They're trying to drill in the Russian Arctic, they're here in the UK, they're drilling in the North Sea…*

LOREN. Across the fog, a silhouette appears. Barnacle. I open my eyes. His shadow seems to reach toward me over the plaza. He beams to me that these things are truly happening, that time is falling off.

What am I supposed to do about it?

Why am I here?

Am I supposed to be your authenticator?

BARNACLE (LOREN *voice-over*). *You will prove that it is real.*

LOREN. No! I am not a cell! I am not a molecule! I'm not an ant, blindly obeying nature! I'M A MODERN MAN!

The ACTOR *picks up a water bottle and throws it at the back wall, shaking the whole space.*

Do you really think Time comes in objects like milk in mothers? You think shuffling around a hundred square miles of bush is supposed to waltz us back across Time? Fuck's sake! Someone has to denounce this, this craziness. I need to start a one-man insurrection. If I'm to survive, I must pump out of my psyche a massively self-generated sense of who I am.

So. Come on. Science. Mathematics. Multiplication tables. One times one is one. One times two is two. One times three is four. No, no, start again. Shut up.

To recapture myself another way, I turn and face the forest. I stare at the green jumble of branches, creepers. Sumaumus. Lupuna.

A new sensation emerges in me, but it is not one of sadness or fresh disaster. I become aware that while I could flee now... I have no interest in doing so. I try to picture myself escaping through the forest, back down the river, getting back to my world... Come on! But escape from what? Into what? What lies ahead is made of the same river, the same plants, but now it's empty of modern humankind. No one like me is out there.

But, listen, the civilised world hasn't disappeared, no, it has simply not appeared yet.

We are the first humans in a territory of unnamed, uncounted life forms. A people taken to the beginning by Barnacle. And I have gone with them.

17. Breakfast at the Dawn of Man

LOREN. Time passes until eventually Cambio stands up and rubs his hands over his face. He lumbers over exhaustedly and sits by me. I close my eyes and open them. Barnacle is standing over us. I look up at him, his stare opaque and sphinx-like. I ask:

Quando vamos morrer?

'When are we going to die?' Cambio translates and Barnacle leans over to tap my arm with his open hand, which feels hard, sure, certain.

'Não morrer,' says Cambio. Not to die. Not to die.

The cold wing of death has lifted, but it's still so close that I feel my hair prickling up on the back of my neck, anticipating its return. My body seems to lose its solid state. I experience a wonderful easing of pressure.

SFX: Barnacle's voice.

Barnacle pulls me to my feet, and then gestures for me to follow him. I do.

He rolls his shoulderblades like an old man fighting stiffness. Two old men. We walk through the forest, to the edge of the river. We both know when to stop. He whispers one word, and I think it means 'look', because he points upstream.

I do look, and an invisible change of lenses seems to occur and my eyes tumble forwards. Five hundred yards extend, while the sound of the water changes. I sense the distant mountains rising beyond the trees.

The beginning is there. The source of the river.

Then from that source comes a message. It is wordless but so gigantic that it breaks all boundaries. It fills all the space outside me, inside me and fuses the source and the beginning into one notion.

Together Barnacle and I beam to each other: *The beginning*.

We face each other.

He explains, still without words, that he cannot let me leave. Not after I have been part of this.

So – you heard me. You know, I whisper without words.

We know, he says. I understand that just as Barnacle undid my spell by running counterclockwise, I could undo their return. I could be the crack between here and there, through which another time, our time, might flood.

He suddenly looks very naked and very tired. Aged, in fact, and vulnerable.

He walks away, back towards the other naked, tired people of the forest.

Until just hours ago, I was a modern man, activated by the pressures of my civilisation, crowded inside its limits. Barnacle and his tribe were pressured by the advance of my civilisation even more, because their only alternative was flight. Their only alternative *is* flight. Yet now the certainty that blooms in every leaf and blade of grass is that we are alone.

Tayah, he calls me by my new name. I nod reassuringly and go to him. Pad back to captivity. The song of the forest rises, gains in richness and melody. My prison, my wonderful prison, is singing.

Forest sounds rise.

18. The Storm

A storm lashes down.

ACTOR. That night a storm shook the trees and rain lashed the canopy so violently that liquid columns of downpour pierced through. Flashes bathed the treetops in an apocalyptic blue light. The water was rising incredibly fast, whipping with unexpected strength at the trees. Swamping their roots. Overflowing the forest floor. It rose with a surge that forced into action all the animals that couldn't count on the trees for protection. They headed for higher ground.

The storm cuts suddenly and the quiet sound of a typewriter replaces it.

LOREN. Caicaque Barnacle. Tribu Matses. Cachoeira Esperanza. Ultra – Oriental Cordillera.

Dear Barnacle,

I don't expect this letter to reach you, and even if it did you couldn't read it without the help of someone like Cambio (Olá Cambio). Still, writing it makes me feel that you are alive.

The storm abruptly cuts over the letter.

ACTOR. McIntyre was almost knocked down by the panicked traffic of tribespeople. He ran into the surrounding trees and found himself in water up to his knees. He was nearly swept off his feet. He was hit in one knee by a floating object, two logs lashed together with palm fibre. He fell across the raft without even thinking of clinging to it, and the current dragged them both through a screen of low branches and beyond. He paddled desperately, trying to steer himself back towards his new family.

But seconds later, the raft had been pulled into the main river and the repeated lightning revealed a frothing, boiling purple mass of water. Return was now impossible. Still, of the thoughts tumbling through his mind, his most anxious was about the headman. Barnacle.

Silence. Then the quiet tapping of typewriter keys.

LOREN. Dear Barnacle,

You are a scientist in your way, as I am in mine. But your attitude is that everything around us is alive and therefore reachable. Nothing is forbidden. That's why you can travel in time.

I want to know about time. I want to know about it. I want to know about the Earth, know about the source of this big river and the natural world it sustains. But for you, it is less important that you know about all these things. What's important is what you do with them. You are doing something with time, rather than agonising about understanding it. That's why I know you are present here and will somehow be able to learn the content of this letter.

SFX: rushing, flowing water.

ACTOR. The morning came fast, the rain seeming to bring a grim grey mass of light down onto the frothing waters. He saw a mudflat, paddled towards it, crawled out and sat for a few moments in the morning light.

And then McIntyre knew, with a certainty that allowed no room for hope or doubt, as if the headman himself was making sure that he had the news, that Barnacle was gone. He was dead, drowned. Barnacle was gone and yet at the same time he was ineradicably present in everything that surrounded him.

So close did he feel to him, that he felt Barnacle's features were somehow superimposed on his own. As if they were one person.

Dying, the headman had exited the daily physical sequence of time, entering instead that space/time/mind continuum McIntyre had experienced. They were travelling in it together.

Then the fantastic sensation, like others so recently experienced, faded.

He staggered out into the water, fell onto his balsa raft and drifted downstream.

Petru recording, played on the ACTOR*'s phone.*

PETRU. *Loren McIntyre died in 2003, and I did not see him before he died. We hadn't lapsed, it simply happened like that, as happens in life with some people that are important, you already know. But then it becomes even more important to remember them, and I was extremely, extremely – I said, why was I so foolish, not to jump on a plane and go see him? But I think I was, er, secretly, frightened to see him weak…*

SFX: typewriter tapping.

LOREN. Dear Barnacle,

I'm here, in Arlington, Virginia, writing to you. I sailed down with the flood, to return to my territory. But I shall return one day to your beginning. Maybe it will only be in my memory, but that will do. Because even there I will learn certain things about you, and you shall learn things about me. And there will be a consequence to our association.

Maybe more people will benefit from it. Or maybe just you and I, sitting near a fire, sharing food, until our thoughts find a way to connect.

ACTOR. Some of us are friends.

This is a conversation between the ACTOR, *live, and Noma McBurney, recorded aged five.*

NOMA. *Dada, I can't sleep.*

ACTOR. Oh sweetie. You've just been up all night. It's only because Mama's not here. You know that.

NOMA. *Will you tell me a story to help me sleep?*

ACTOR. I've told you one already.

NOMA. *One from the book you're reading.*

ACTOR. It's a grown-up book, sweetie. It's not for children.

NOMA. *Dada, please read me a story.*

ACTOR. Okay. I'll find something in here…

NOMA. *One from the book you're reading.*

ACTOR. Yes, okay. This is a story about the beginning of a people. The Mayoruna people. You're at the beginning, aren't you, sweetie?

NOMA. *Yes.*

ACTOR. This is the story of how they began. It's a story from Petru's book. You remember Petru, don't you, sweetie?

NOMA. *Yes.*

ACTOR. Well, it was told to Petru by a man called McIntyre, and it was told to him by Cambio. And Cambio heard it from his father. And his father heard it from his father…

Once upon a time, the big river flowed in the sky. Its whole valley was carried on clouds, fastened to the clouds with bulky liana ropes. Many people lived in the valley in the sky in perfect harmony. But one day a curious bunch of children untied one of the ropes. That was enough to undo the whole:

rope after rope snapped under the pressure, and the valley crashed onto the earth. Thus the big river split into thousands of smaller rivers, and the sky, sad over the loss, cried its first rain.

Some of us are friends. (*Looped.*)

The sound of Noma breathing, asleep.

The End.

A Nick Hern Book

The Encounter first published in Great Britain in 2016 as a paperback original by Nick Hern Books Limited, The Glasshouse, 49a Goldhawk Road, London W12 8QP, in association with Complicite

Adapted from the novel *Amazon Beaming* by Petru Popescu, republished by Pushkin Press in 2016

The Encounter copyright © 2016 Complicite

Front cover image: Simon McBurney © Gianmarco Bresadola

Designed and typeset by Nick Hern Books, London
Printed in Great Britain by CPI Books (UK) Ltd

A CIP catalogue record for this book is available from the British Library

ISBN 978 1 84842 554 5

MIX
Paper from
responsible sources
FSC   FSC® C013604
www.fsc.org